VOLUME 4   BOO-CEN

THE PRACTICAL ENCYCLOPEDIA OF

Good Decorating

and Home Improvement

GREYSTONE PRESS

Alphabetically arranged and fully illustrated, your *Practical Encyclopedia of Good Decorating and Home Improvement* has been planned for your convenience and immediate use. In feature articles you will find a wealth of facts, ideas, suggestions, and advice that will help you solve your decorating problems. A Master/Guide at the back of each volume includes concise articles of historical interest, definitions of terms, and summaries of feature articles in the volume. Helpful cross-references appear throughout all volumes. On many pages you will find illustrations and descriptions of Project Plans and Home Plans, identified by the abbreviations PP and HP. For complete information on these plans write to Good Decorating Plans Editor, Greystone Press, 225 Park Avenue South, New York, N.Y. 10003.

(Continued from page 558, Volume 3.)

Highlight bookshelves with accessories

Row upon row of books makes a handsome and impressive sight, but there's no unwritten law that says you have to put only books on your shelves. Because they are open, bookcases and bookshelves are meant for display as well as storage, and they are ideal spots to show off collections. Planned with thought and an eye toward good balance, a bookcase or a wall of shelves filled with books and accessories can be a striking center of interest.

When planning a display you will want to select accessories to blend with the style theme of your rooms. Interspersed with books, almost any accessory or souvenir you own is suitable for display somewhere in your home.

In a living room, you might use vases, plants, pictures, candlesticks, figurines, or

This handsome unit is a well-balanced combination of storage areas for things that should be out of sight and shelves for things that should be seen. Books have been artfully grouped and placed in blocks so that their vertical lines punctuate the expanses of white. An eclectic assortment of accessories has been thoughtfully arranged to show each one to its best advantage. Note how well the shapes and colors suit the shelf spaces.

Below, a series of shelves suspended from metal wall strips by brackets forms a pattern on the wall, and books have been combined with accessories to make a decorative center of interest. Painting the wall behind shelves in a bright color, as here, is often a good idea, focusing attention on the design and accessories. For extra strength and solidity, these shelves were notched to receive the points of the brackets.

Notice how the books are arranged—some in an upright position, larger reference books lying on their sides, smaller books piled up to serve as bookends. Such an arrangement not only is useful but adds variety and interest to the overall composition. The shelves were finished to blend with other furniture woods in the room, an easy job to do at home.

small sculptures. Tureens, platters, or a collection of goblets or wine glasses that you use occasionally are especially appropriate display pieces in a dining room. Ornamental trays, decanters, and fine china plates are suitable in either a living room or a dining room.

Less formal accessories and collections are good display pieces in a den or much-used family room. Games, puzzles, records, and even sports equipment such as tennis rackets and football helmets can be attractively arranged on your bookshelves. Aquariums and goldfish bowls are happy accents in all informal rooms.

Kitchens and bathrooms are good places for bookshelves too. In a kitchen you might display a collection of mugs, canisters, spice jars, or antique utensils on the shelves with your cookbooks, and in a bathroom a collection of jars, boxes, shells, or rocks can be effectively teamed with a small plant or two and some books.

These are only a few suggestions of accessories you might choose to display with your

◄Encourage study with a library corner such as the one at left. It has everything—built-in cabinets for storage, neatly arranged bookshelves laden with books for reference and study (as well as some fiction and general works for escapist reading), a globe, a comfortable chair, and a good desk with space for files and stationery. Fluorescent lighting, installed over the recessed shelves, makes titles easy to find and supplements natural light from the window.

At right is an idea for planning shelves to match your style theme. Instead of sleekly functional metal strips and brackets, the designer of these shelves used antique Spanish corbels, or supports, and antiqued walnut for the shelves themselves. Placement was planned to incorporate the old chest and the painting into the overall composition. A search of junkyards or secondhand stores can turn up interesting supports that can be antiqued with an easy-to-use kit.

Ordinary shelving and metal support fixtures are the basis of the charming kitchen wall shown below. Underneath a collection of cookbooks, a tilted rack holds the latest home improvement magazines for coffee-time browsing. Toys, a set of mugs, a copper mold—things that are used occasionally or often—are displayed in easy-to-reach places, and infrequently used books line the bottom shelf. Glass jars containing canned fruit and vegetables serve as bookends. They are especially appropriate accent pieces on kitchen shelves—decorative, functional, and handy for cooking.

books. You have only to let your imagination roam to think of dozens of others.

The personal touch

Before you start arranging accessories and books, stop and think of the treasured things you own and may have tucked away in a drawer or cupboard somewhere. Dig them out and see if they are suitable for display. Maybe you still have your first doll or the first model airplane you ever made or an old high-school trophy you once won. Such souvenirs can bring back pleasant memories if they are where you can see them every day.

Many mementoes of bygone years are suitable for framing and displaying on your bookshelves. A wedding invitation, a report card from the third grade, a sampler that your mother worked in cross-stitch, a diploma, or an old certificate of merit—all are potential decorative accessories. Included among your books they can add a very personal touch to your home, recalling the past of the people who live there.

Here's an idea for some extra book space you may not realize you have. In the room shown at left was a doorway that was seldom used, because there was plenty of access to the adjoining room through other doors. So this doorway was blocked up and recessed bookshelves were installed, to add glamour to the stairway and help focus attention on its unusual treatment. A bonus—the adjoining room gained wall space for better furniture arrangement. Here the edges of the shelves are painted in a pale tone to match the walls, give horizontal continuity. The carpet color is picked up for the inside of the shelves and the uprights, to establish yet another color relationship. Because the shelves are recessed, they are safe for the display of fragile accessories, since there is little chance that a stray elbow can knock them off.

Another bright idea is the handrail, made of theatrical cord color-matched to the carpet and the bookshelves, and following the graceful curve of the stairway. It is draped through brass fixtures that pick up a highlight of the bookcase accessories. Notice, too, that the pictures are hung to be a part of the bookcase-handrail composition, lined up with the top of the shelves, and with frames and mats in blending color.

At left, below, a caned free-standing shelf unit of delicate and formal line conforms to the traditional styling of the room, repeats the caning of the armchair back, and at the same time gives an airy feeling, a sense of space. Here, it combines book and accessory display with a serving-center top that is adequate for buffets in a small room. The wall above is accessorized with pictures and a planter in an informal arrangement. Notice that the candlesticks thrust upward to become a part of this grouping, and that the candles themselves repeat and accentuate the color of the picture mats.

You can adapt this idea to a spot in your own home in almost any style you desire. The legs and uprights of the unit can be turnings for a formal or country look, painted or antiqued to blend with your color and furnishings theme. Brass or aluminum legs would be more suitable for a contemporary room. Instead of caning, ordinary expanded metal painted to blend or contrast with the legs is both sturdy and handsome. You will need metal-cutting tools for this.

Flanking a dramatic white fireplace that is the center of ▶ interest of the room at right, twin units of shelves hold a variety of books and accessories. The units are not identical twins—they are just enough alike to be balanced and just enough different to be interesting. Set off by the bold green background, they provide space for display and storage of books, art objects, souvenirs, records, and a television set.

The entire wall was designed as one large composition, unified by the background color and the shelving, and it serves as a combination bookcase and entertainment center. Note that shelves are of various widths and heights, exactly suitable for the objects displayed. Such a custom look is not difficult to achieve with adjustable fixtures; they cannot be recommended to the home decorator too highly.

One or two tilted shelves are always a good idea in planning a wall arrangement similar to this one. They are particularly useful for holding recent issues of magazines, and they permit you to display some of your books so that the front covers show. Oversize books with handsome dust-jackets are effectively displayed this way, adding a different look from the normal upright view.

BORDERS

Add Accent And Variety To Your Decorating Scheme With Borders

You can use borders to good effect in almost any decorating scheme—formal or informal, traditional or modern—in any room in your home. Whether paint, paper, or fabric, they will give a custom-made look wherever they are used. A wide variety of durable wall materials and colorful fabric tapes is available in most department stores.

Use borders to set off objects or areas you want to emphasize, or to create a series of related shapes to give a room unity. A border defines areas much as picture frames do. Print borders break the monotony of continuous areas of solid colors. Solid-color borders work in just the opposite optical way to break up and relieve the busyness of a large patterned

A sophisticated black-and-white scroll pattern on woven tape trims a folding screen of plywood covered in brilliantly colored fabric; it also decorates the matching valance above the window in the adjoining dining-room area. In addition to adding drama and a sharp color contrast, the screen deftly separates.

To prove that a good idea bears repeating, a wider version of the same border is used to trim a living-room sofa pillow, thus coordinating the scheme.

The basic decorating idea illustrated here is usable in many situations, but it is especially suited to the rented home or apartment. As screens are not attached to the wall, they may be moved from one place to another, or re-covered to suit the color scheme of a later home.

As the close-up of the border pattern shows, it resembles a cross-stitch embroidery design. It could be duplicated on a larger scale by any homemaker who enjoys using her own needlework to enhance the decorating theme of her home. Border designs may also be used to trim lampshades and table linens such as place mats and napkins.

area. If you choose a print, a small, simple design is usually best, as it will not stand out enough to conflict with others in the room.

Walls are a traditional place for borders, but you need not limit your ideas of wall borders to those near the ceiling. You can create a fake chair rail with a border, or you can simulate a dado by painting the lower part of a wall and adding a border. You can even put borders on your baseboards.

There are literally dozens of decorative ways to use borders on furnishings. Painted or applied bordering can transform an unattractive chest of drawers into a distinctive piece of furniture. A plain lamp shade can be made much more interesting with the simple addition of a colorful strip at or near the bottom. You can appliqué borders on curtains, on bedspreads, and on rugs. Use them to make your draperies more elegant or to emphasize the shape of valances and cornices. Paint them on cupboard doors, glue them on wastepaper baskets, on window shades, on the bathtub. Once you take a look around with borders on your mind, you will discover just what a versatile decorating device they are.

The kaleidoscope motif of the vinyl flooring of the room above was used as a border on range, refrigerator, dishwasher, and cupboards, adding an Old World touch to modern appliances. If you live in an apartment or a rented house that needs brightening up, patterned borders such as this one are an easy way to relieve the antiseptic whiteness of rented kitchens and bathrooms. Similar patterns are available in inexpensive paper and fabric tapes in most hardware stores.

The decorating plan of the bedroom at left was keyed to the striking border of the all-wool, handcrafted area rug. The floral motif is repeated in the hand-printed cotton panels on the wall behind the beds and in the appliquéd designs on the bedspreads. Borders of olive green outline the panels and edge both bedspreads and bolsters. Note that the small, busy pattern of the wallpaper and the bold floral motif are offset by a liberal use of solid green and white.

How To Make Your Boy's Room Rugged And Easy To Maintain

Decorating a boy's room must be done with the boy in mind. Forget this and you might end up with a room more suited to a girl.

But some mothers who plan decorating for their sons' rooms don't seem to pay proper attention to this important difference. By using too-light colors and fragile furniture and fabrics, they cause themselves needless work and expense. And—just as important—they fail to create the pleasantly masculine air that a boy wants in his retreat.

It simply is not his nature to think in advance what propping feet comfortably on a bedspread will produce in wrinkles and soil. How much more sensible to have a bedspread that will not wrinkle easily and that is patterned or dark enough so minor spots won't show. And let it be a washable spread that can be popped into the machine when the time comes.

Older boys like to be consulted about colors and patterns that are to be used in decorating their rooms. And although they may rebel at going on a shopping trip, most would enjoy looking over some fabric swatches and indicating preferences of colors and patterns they are to live with.

When it comes to furniture selection, it is wise to remember that little boys grow into big boys sooner than you'd think. So keep the future in mind and avoid pieces that have too much "nursery" flavor and so will soon be outgrown. Sectionals are a fine solution for families on the move, so that pieces can be rearranged to fit new space.

Do not overlook the need for some display space where a boy can show off his collection of toy soldiers and trains at first and later, perhaps, pennants, fishing lures, or souvenirs of vacation travels. Bookcases, with some shelves reserved for his display, are suited for many such collections. Bulletin boards, too, may accommodate some.

Encourage good study habits with a comfortable desk and chair. The desk drawers should be roomy enough to store all of his school supplies.

Good lighting both for the desk area and general illumination of the room is important. Built-in lighting fixtures are ideal here, since they don't take up floor space, won't be accidentally knocked over, can be placed where they will put best light on books and papers. Lamps that fasten to the wall and swing out of the way are also desirable, and are easy to find in styles that suit male tastes.

For floor covering, avoid small rugs that kick up. Choose durable, easy-to-clean, hard- or soft-finish material that can "take it."

Lavish use of orange for walls and floor covering dominates ▶ a masculine color scheme that also includes bright blue and yellow. Generous work surface and lots of cupboards and drawers for storing study or hobby materials neatly out of sight should be an encouragement to good housekeeping habits in a boy.

Hobby interest in trains is attractively expressed by the wall-mounted model of an old steam engine, and by the pattern of fabric used to make a bedspread that won't show every spot. The bookshelves display other hobby interests and memorabilia of the sort boys like to collect.

Sectional furniture of the kind used here makes good sense for a boy's room, both because it takes less floor space than would the equivalent freestanding furniture, and because it makes possible later rearrangement of pieces or their removal should the family move to another home. Built-ins are also well suited for furnishing a boy's room, but they can't go along when a move is made.

Let him help with the decorating

If there is one hue your boy definitely prefers, start with it and add complementary or companion colors to create a happy atmosphere.

If he has a hobby that requires lots of equipment, try to provide for it in the furnishings and built-in storage of his own bedroom. Get him to sit down with you and list the kinds and quantities of supplies he'll want handy, and help in sketching a floor plan that will accommodate the essentials.

If he's a collector—and what boy is not—plan shelves or wall boards where he can display some of his choicest possessions.

For an older boy who is a camera enthusiast and likes to develop his own photographs, here's the ideal setup. The recessed section, with good counter space above and cupboards below, holds all the equipment he'll need to pursue his hobby; it can be converted to a darkroom by closing a sliding door out of camera view at right.

The ceiling-height soffit makes an attractive display spot for showing off favorite photographs and puts a touch of bright yellow in the room, which is otherwise furnished and paneled in maple, with blue carpeting and paint trim for accent.

Comfortable study corner includes desk space, wall-hung bookshelves, ample drawer space, and a desk light that can be raised for overall lighting in that corner of the room, or lowered to focus on books and papers when he's working at the desk.

If his room space and your budget permit, it's a wonderful aid to good family relations to let a young man have his own television set in his room, to be tuned in to his favorite programs without need for elaborate negotiations. Here, a small portable rests on top of a section of drawers at left of the desk.

Crisply contemporary in its blue-green color scheme, this room for a teen-ager has bunkbeds so that an overnight guest can be accommodated on occasion without sacrificing the floor space twin beds would require. The colorful furniture is relatively low in cost but sturdy enough to withstand lots of wear. The wall-to-wall carpeting in solid green makes an average-size room look larger.

This unusual window treatment is worth noticing, as it is a style adaptable to a wide variety of uses. In this case, the striped fabric that sets the color scheme for the entire room is mounted on a roller so that it may be raised and lowered like the conventional window shade. Used here by itself, it could also be combined attractively with tailored draperies in other settings.

The new shade fabrics now on the market and new methods of installation make them increasingly popular. They range from light-without-glare to completely darkening styles. Fabric of your selection can be laminated to standard shades.

Young families living in small houses will be interested in the problem-solving bedroom scheme below. It works in any 9 x 12-foot room, and with a decor like this one, it's bound to please any two young boys who like the sailor's life.

The shelf-desk unit consists of a three-drawer file cabinet (buy it, or build one from 3/4-inch plywood or 1/10-inch pine) and a plywood slab to be painted or covered with formica as a desk top. Two legs support the desk at the open end. (Legs, too, may be purchased in a variety of heights and styles.) Side-mounted shelf stripping over the desk makes shelf installation easy. The captain's chair with bright canvas seat and back is attractive, inexpensive.

Hard-surface vinyl flooring is an economical choice because it is both durable and easy to clean—an important consideration when occupants are apt to spill paints or foods.

To build bed frames like these, first measure the dimensions of children's box springs and mattresses. Add an inch to each measurement to get the inside dimensions of bunk boxes. (The springs fit flush inside bunk units, mattresses atop.) Now construct sturdy frames to your dimensions, using 2 x 4s. You may require some professional help with the built-in drawers under the bunks, but such drawers are great for stowing toys, bedding, or clothing.

Cover the bunk frames with 1/2- to 3/4-inch plywood. The tugboat-size ship's wheel and yellow rope for the divider came from a marine supply company, as did the porthole and ship's bell overhead. Sailcloth or canvas would make sturdy bedspreads and draperies.

The sunny yellow-orange hues, combined with lots of white, make this a room children will be happy in.

A tailored look in room furnishings will suit a young man. He'll introduce his own "accents," depending on his interests of the moment. Mod posters, maps, travel ads are but a few of the colorful wall decorations he may choose.

In the late teens, he'll probably want to have his room redecorated, erasing any leftover suggestions of the child he used to be. If basic furniture was chosen with an eye to the future, it probably will not need to be replaced. New draperies, bedspread, and floor covering and a change of wall color can work wonders.

Designed for a college man, the room at right is planned as ▶ his own private retreat, away from distracting family activities. Once a breezeway, this small remodeled room presented a real decorating challenge.

It was effectively met by using crisp contemporary furnishings that are sturdily constructed, scaled to the smaller room, and largely wall-hung to provide maximum storage and performance without taking up large amounts of floor space.

For senior high men, a good study spot, well lighted, is a must. This simple desk and auxiliary closet take up the entire length of a 12-foot wall. The units actually add to usable floor space by doing the jobs of several pieces of furniture.

The desk hangs from studs in the walls behind it and on either side so there's plenty of room underneath for long legs. (A virtue of wall-hung furniture is that it can be raised as the user grows up and comfortable desk height changes.)

Strip lighting under the shelves plus the wall-mounted fixture supply good illumination for the desk as well as general light for the room. Shelves mounted on adjustable strips allow alterations in spaces between to accommodate books and other items a young man likes to display.

Let him help choose the room scheme from a selection of paint chips and swatches of fabric. Then, when the decorating is done, he'll feel it's truly his room.

Gain floor space with built-ins

Young boys want floor space where they can spread out games, coloring books, building blocks, and toys. But how do you provide it in a bedroom for two that measures only 12 × 12 feet and must also contain essential beds, storage, and desks?

Custom-built furnishings are the answer, as you can see from the floor plan and picture below, or furniture that you build yourself.

With quarters like this, boys will be happy to play in their room, leave the living room tidy and available for adults' use.

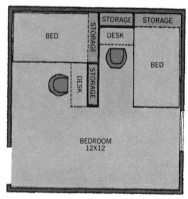

Until you examine the floor plan shown above, it's hard to believe that it's possible to get two beds, two desks, and all that storage into such a small space, leaving half of a 12 x 12-foot bedroom free for active play by two youngsters.

There's another advantage to the way this furniture is constructed and arranged: each boy has privacy when he's studying. (For a complete Project Plan, order PP 3603-2.)

Complementary color scheme of blue and orange has a masculine vitality about it that most boys will like. Painted furniture is inexpensive to make, sturdy, and easy to repaint if it gets scuffed or a change of color scheme is wanted.

The colorful bedding on today's market is attractive enough so that sheets and blankets can become integral parts of a decorating scheme. For a bunkbed setup like this, spreads really aren't necessary to everyday good looks, and eliminating them will save both money and bed-making time.

Colored sheets like those used on the beds can also be used effectively to make tailored curtains, carrying the color scheme into the other half of the room.

Provide the right kind of storage space

How to stow gear is a problem faced by all parents of young—and not so young—boys. Unless their rooms are equipped with an ample amount of storage space, arranged for fast "ins and outs," there is bound to be a perpetual clutter, to say nothing of time wasted trying to find things.

Lots of shallow drawers and shelves are a much better answer than deep ones. They let you see at a glance what's there, make it possible to put things of one kind in one place, make maximum use of space.

For the very young, picture symbols attached to shelves and drawers will help a great deal to teach good storage habits.

The closet above, well arranged to suit a young boy's needs, shows how to make every inch of storage space count. It's divided into sections planned to fit specific items to be stored. It includes rods for hanging jackets and trousers, with no wasted space. Shelves hold headgear, suitcases, and camping equipment. Door rack keeps neckties and belts neatly available. Many shallow drawers will take the rest of his wardrobe.

Although this particular closet arrangement is custom-built, it's possible to have an almost identical arrangement without hiring a skilled carpenter to do the installation. Purchase an unpainted chest of drawers of the dimensions that will take maximum advantage of space available in your closet. Install a series of shelves supported by triangular braces that attach to a closet wall. Your lumber dealer will cut lengths of boards to any measurements you wish. Paint the chest and shelves to harmonize with room colors.

Bright idea in this bedroom for two young boys is the installation of perforated wallboard, which turns stored items into decorations. They're in plain view, can be taken down for use, replaced on wallboard with little effort.

Such a plan makes it possible to install a series of shelves very easily, should there be a larger number of things requiring shelf storage. Or the shelves could hold school books as boys grow up and want reference material handy.

Series of drawers serve both as support for desk tops and as storage for toys and clothing. Bunkbeds free floor space so children can spread out toys and games. Wall-to-wall carpeting in a color that doesn't show soil easily has practical good looks and helps to carry out the room scheme set by attractive plaid spreads.

BRAND NAMES

What To Consider Before Investing Your Decorating Dollars

Brand names are recognized guideposts to quality. This simple fact is often overlooked by prospective homeowners and purchasers of major items of household equipment.

When you buy a new home or remodel an older one, and purchase new furnishings and major appliances, you're investing in a number of large-expense items. It is absolutely essential that all materials and equipment be well made and that they give you long and dependable service in years to come.

Among the estimated half-million-plus families who will buy new homes this year, there are certain to be thousands who'll come to grief and lose money because they don't pay sufficient attention to brand names. Most of these people wouldn't consider purchasing an X-brand television set or automobile. But they often ignore brands when buying a home—probably the biggest single purchase they'll ever make, as well as the one they'll expect to last longest.

Fortunately, brand names and builder reliability usually go hand in hand. There are exceptions, of course. But as a rule, builders who stick to brand-name products throughout their houses are the men who stay in business.

Exactly what do brand names mean? In most new homes or remodelings, they mean four distinct advantages:

(1) *You get uniform quality,* wherever you shop—from appliance store to building materials outlet (although you'll find variety in grades and models). Also, you can be as confident about the products you buy for your home in Springfield, Ohio, as you can in Springfield, Massachusetts.

(2) *Products will be more dependable.* Windows that are designed to open easily usually will do so. If a maker says his shingles will last 15 years, they will. After spending large sums of money establishing a brand name, the manufacturer can't afford to turn out slipshod products. Of course, this is not universally true, but your chances of getting reliable performance with brand-name products are excellent; with off-brands, you're taking what could be a very costly risk, especially when you take into account the extra charges for installing a replacement.

(3) *When you're given a warranty* on products bearing a brand name, it will be a clear, concise statement of the terms set by the maker—and he'll back those terms.

(4) *When parts wear out, or adjustment is needed, service is available.* Often the service branch will be nearby and—even more important—it will be functioning. Some years ago a group of homes in Florida featured aluminum jalousie doors on the front and back entries. Six months after the homes were completed, nearly 40 percent of the doors proved defective. A homeowner committee tried to reach the manufacturer—a local firm. The plant was empty, and not one of the company officials had left a forwarding address when he moved.

Even though many local firms do a fine, craftsmanlike production job, few can offer you all four brand-name advantages as listed above. So, if every building dollar counts, insist on brand names all through the home before you make the deal and avoid paying later for costly mistakes.

BREAKFAST ROOMS

Serve Your Morning Meals In An Inviting Eating Area

Little touches often add up to big decorating, supplying the sparkle and liveliness needed to make a room inviting. The breakfast room below was designed to relieve morning meals of monotony. Instant scenery does the trick. In a small, windowless space at one end of the kitchen, wallpaper with a bamboo design creates the feeling of an indoor gazebo. Paper was cut to form the arch, then the edge was painted to match segments of the latticed pattern. A lavabo filled with green fern and the chairs continue the garden theme.

One of the most popular family gathering places in any home is a cozy eating area in or near the kitchen. It's a handy place to serve breakfast, informal meals, and snacks or coffee when friends drop in.

If you don't have a separate room that can be turned into a breakfast room, use your imagination. A large kitchen can be broken into separate areas, each with its own motif and purpose. A bar, work-area cabinets, a painted screen, or a rail fence can add character and interest as well as dividing the space for practical purposes.

It's wise to follow the same general decorating theme in a breakfast area as in the kitchen, but you can easily vary it by using unique accents. Touches of individuality will set cooking and dining areas apart.

A breakfast room is the place to use a favorite color, a bright wallpaper pattern, unusual accessories. You can choose from an array of new wall and flooring materials and window fabrics—all made to withstand the rigors of kitchen wear.

Don't forget the importance of cheerful lighting. Through winter months when it's dark and gloomy at breakfast time, you can make your own sunshine with an interesting fixture or concealed lighting.

Splashes of cheerful color, an amusing light fixture, and ▶ attractive and comfortably cushioned chairs transform a small space at one end of a kitchen into a charming breakfast room.

An unusual window treatment (especially effective if an outlook is unattractive) uses gauzy fabric of an allover geometric pattern in yellow. The top half is a simple, pleated valance. The bottom half suggests shutters, with shirred fabric on rods concealed behind the hinged frames, which open to let outer windows be raised or lowered.

A Hundred And One Ways
To Achieve Beauty On A Budget

Inviting rooms, that say "Welcome" to all who enter, are not limited to those who have a generous decorating budget. Even though you have a very modest amount of money to spend on furnishing and decorating your home, you can create an atmosphere that is inviting, comfortable, and personal—and still stay within the limits of your budget.

Home is, after all, the setting for yourself and your family. So let it reflect your skills, talents, interests. If it does that meaningfully, it's bound to be attractive.

One good approach is to start with a floor plan for the room or area that you want to decorate or redecorate. List all the items to be purchased, and all the jobs to be done in the process of furnishing and decorating. Then study your list carefully and pick out those you might be able to do yourself.

One of the most efficient ways to stretch decorating dollars and get the most value from your expenditures is to buy one or more really good pieces of furniture, and then rely on your ingenuity and elbow-grease to fill in the gaps until you can afford to buy the rest of the luxury-priced pieces you eventually want to get.

Perhaps you'll decide that a well-constructed and fashionably upholstered sofa is to be the one "luxury" item in your living room. If so, subtract its price from the total amount you've decided you can spend on the living room, and use the remainder to purchase used pieces that can be inexpensively refinished, or unfinished furniture that you can paint or antique yourself. Be sure to include the cost of paint, lumber, and fabric in the cost of the budget pieces. With this approach, you can produce an atmosphere of freshness, convenience, and decorating appeal.

The principle holds true for one room or the entire home. If it is the bedroom that demands your attention, the big investment will probably be the box spring and mattress. You can use your ingenuity to create an unusual headboard, refinish a secondhand chest, and paint a desk or table and a chair. If your problem area is the dining room, you may decide to spend most of the room allowance on a table and chairs. If so, the remainder can be used for a secondhand chest or buffet that can be restored and refinished.

Later, as your budget permits, you can replace the make-do pieces with furnishings you want to live with permanently. On the other hand, you may be pleasantly surprised to find that your "budget treatments" are the most effective items in your overall decorating scheme.

If you are not completely confident that you have the skill and the ingenuity to carry out successful decorating projects, start out with one that is inexpensive and not too complex.

The three-dimensional wall treatment at right gives an expansive feeling to a small room. First, paint the wall opposite the most-used doorway in a solid color. When the surface is thoroughly dry, apply 18-inch-wide panels of adhesive-backed vinyl. Overlap the corners at first, work out all air bubbles, then cut away the corners as shown here, using a razor blade and a straightedge. Carefully remove a 1-inch strip from each mitered corner to reveal the wall color and add to the three-dimensional effect. As a finishing touch, hang a few shapely straw mats. Furniture painted in a contrasting color and a ceiling droplight fixture of simple design enhance the contemporary effect of the room.

The old saying "nothing ventured, nothing gained" is very much to the point for anyone who holds back from starting a redecorating or home-improvement plan. You may have doubts about your ability to carry out the overall changes your home seems to need. If you start with a small project and follow it through to successful completion, however, you will often gain the confidence you need to undertake larger, more expensive projects.

The fear of investing a sizable sum of money and then being dissatisfied with the result is a natural one. Most of us live with

This space-saver for a teen-ager is a compact three-in-one unit, 30 inches high by 20 inches long. It provides a desk, a night table, a vanity—and plenty of storage space. To make one like it, you will need a three-drawer unfinished, unassembled chest; a set of four spacers; two legs; scraps of lumber and plywood, and a 20 × 80-inch door to form the top. All are available from a lumber dealer. For the door, you could substitute ¾-inch plywood and cover it with laminated vinyl for a really fast job. Paint the unit to coordinate with the colors in bed coverlets or in the general room scheme.

It cost less than $15 to create this attractive and useful telephone center. The wall-hung desk is the top part of an old school desk that was bought at auction. Under the lid are stored the telephone directory, scratch pads, lists, whatever you like to have at hand when making telephone calls. The stool, purchased new and unfinished, was painted in a bright color keyed to the wallpaper design. When the phone is not in use and the stool is tucked under the desk, the tiny space required could be spared from almost any kitchen or hall.

our decorating mistakes once we make them. The armoire that looked so elegant at an antique auction may become an ungainly white elephant that dwarfs your bedroom; the bright yellow wallpaper that seemed so cheery at first may be a blinding nightmare after a month in your kitchen. If only a small sum is involved, however, mistakes don't seem so terrible. At least, a low-cost error is better than an expensive one.

For less than $25, you can duplicate many of the decorating projects described and pictured in this chapter. Some are designed primarily to add convenience to your home, some are purely decorative, and some are both. All of them are easy on the budget and just as effective as they are economical. Most of them are even fun to do.

None of the projects calls for more than the minimal skill required to wield a paintbrush, use the tools designed for handyman carpentry, or execute simple sewing techniques. Each suggestion is adaptable to many different versions; with slight modifications, each project can fit your decorating theme.

If you're on "dead center" about changing the decorations of your home, consider the ideas illustrated in this chapter as a good and inexpensive way to begin, and thus build confidence in your own ability.

These mushroom stools and the bracketed shelf cost about $60. To make a pair of sturdy little stools, pick up four tire rims from a junkyard and have them welded into two units; paint the bases to harmonize with your color scheme. Cover circular foam cushions with felt, and add contrasting trim. Use rubber cement to secure the fabric to the cushions. Paint the shelf unit, then seal with flat lacquer. For a spatter effect, flick with benzine glaze solution applied to surface with blunt brush. Add a strip to the inner edge, and apply a final coat of lacquer to preserve your handiwork.

Dollar-wise decorating

Little touches can add up to big effects in decorating. They can supply the sparkle and liveliness needed to give a drab room a newly imaginative air. And their effectiveness bears little relation to their cost.

How is it done? In as many ways as your imagination can turn up. This is not to say you should simply sit down, stare into the surrounding space, and wait for a completely new idea to enter your mind. You can "prime" your imagination by learning to look at photographs throughout this series with an eye to observing more than just the major feature of decoration that is under discussion.

For instance, in a room that is featured for its distinctive floor covering, or its wall treatment, you may see accessory ideas that appeal to you. An expensive-looking, custom-made chest might inspire you to hunt out a piece with similar lines in a resale shop and refinish it in a way that suits your style of decorating. Thus you might gain an attractive and useful item with only a small investment.

◀The tic-tac-toe dart board at upper left on the opposite page can be built for about $6. Glue nine cork tiles in an alternating pattern onto a base of scrap plywood. Stain the frame.

The brilliantly colored folding screen to the right of the dart board costs about $20 to make. Start with two 24-inch hollow-core doors. Cover the entire surface with one coat of white shellac. Divide the doors into sections and paint them in different colors, separating the sections with contrasting tape. Finally, hinge the doors together.

The handsome headboard at lower left can be assembled from ten 12 × 16-inch stock picture frames with cove molding. Cut quilted fabric so that the pattern is the same in all openings. Leave an excess cloth border and tape it to inserts that go inside the frames. Secure the frames to a ¼-inch plywood backing with screws from the back.

The brightly patterned rug can be made from ordinary bathroom carpets. Cut matching patterns from two different colored, one-toned rugs marked on the back. Alternate the colors and stitch together. Glue 2-inch burlap strips over back seams and add yarn fringe.

The basket stack at right provides storage, enables you to display favorite accessories, and adds a splash of color. Cut shelves 22 × 14½ inches from ¾-inch plywood. Seal the edges with wood filler and paint to blend with your room. Hang the shelves on decorative metal brackets.

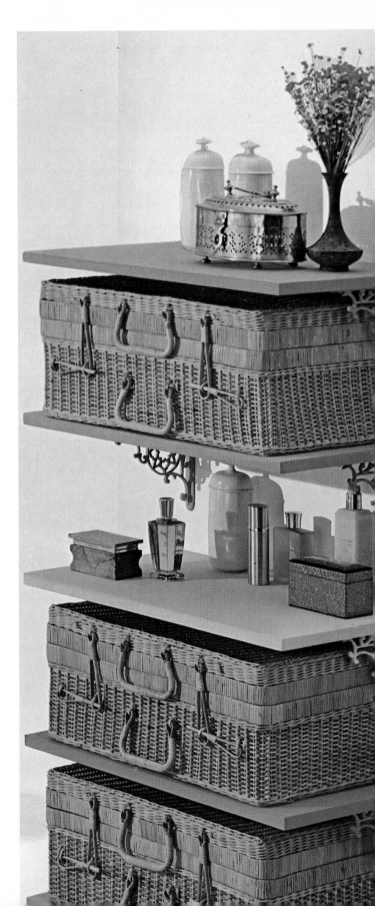

There is nothing drab about an entry hall whose white walls serve as a setting for a Chinese-red desk and matching staircase woodwork.

One way to make a little count for a lot in decorating is to capitalize upon an element of surprise. Here, the surprise is to find a desk of such classic lines painted in so unconventional a hue.

An ordinary chest of drawers that needed refinishing gained distinction in the process.

To achieve the interesting tortoiseshell effect, apply three different shades of bright green paint diluted with benzine to a watery consistency. Here, four coats of the thinned paint were needed to cover.

For a subtle glow, use clear lacquer as a final coat. For contrast, spray the drawer pulls and knobs with white enamel.

The cheapest way to brighten your room

The generous use of bright color is the greatest part of many a room-brightening plan that can be carried out by budget decorators who have more time than money at their disposal. Paint and paper—if you will do the application—are the least expensive ingredients of any project.

Walls, woodwork, and furniture all take on a newer, smarter air if they are drawn into the scheme with cheerful color.

Beginners have the best possibility for success when they limit colors to two—one dominant, the other used as an accent. If you feel that your two-color scheme lacks punch, count on a touch or two of black to sharpen it up in a hurry.

Remember, too, that the fresh green of plants blends well with any color scheme.

Look-alive room accents can spice up a bland decor and stay within the price limits of a slim budget; the secret is *color*.

If you plan to redecorate one—or more than one—room in your home because it seems to lack appeal and personality, take a second look before you plunge into a total redecorating project. Is the deficiency primarily a lack of bold color?

If your answer is "yes," perhaps you need only add a few accents to change the scene.

Color is a bargain in any decorating plan, since it costs no more to have furnishings of vivid hues than of bland ones.

You can, of course, overdo color. A nice balance between the neutral and the vivid elements of the total scheme is what you seek. If floors and/or walls are neutral, look to furniture and fabrics for an essential color contrast. If furnishings are mostly of earth tones, perhaps you should introduce a wall of color.

Because major items of furniture and floor coverings are relatively costly ingredients in a decorating scheme, they should be among the last items you consider replacing when you

The old trunk in the room below, reconditioned and reinforced, serves as a distinctive coffee table, adding needed character to the setting. The panel surfaces of the trunk have been painted and antiqued to match the dark leather of the couches. Large homemade floor cushions substitute for extra pull-up chairs that may be acquired later. The platform along the back wall and the large white box concealing the television set were constructed from 2 × 12-inch planks.

Note the unusual door pulls on the cabinet. The small stand at left of the fireplace is a wooden box painted white. Secondhand stores have many curious items such as the old iron brazier to the right of the hearth, imaginatively used here to hold fire logs. The dark, wide-planked floor and stripped-brick firewall emphasize the rustic warmth of the room, while the steep pitch of the roof is de-emphasized by white walls and ceiling.

For a room with few windows, or windows facing east or north, the sun colors add a feeling of warmth. And they team well with white or black backgrounds and accents.

When choosing colors, remember that the bold, warm hues tend to make space appear smaller, whereas the cool ones create an optical illusion of greater size. If you want to use warm hues in a small room, however, you can still do so effectively if you use them as accents rather than as major elements (walls and floors) in the decor.

Our eyes accept pale colors without shock. These tones seem to allow the eye to look past and through. So use pastels to increase apparent room size. If the ceiling is too low, white or pale tints will give the impression of greater height. Light walls and floor covering can make a room appear both spacious and airy.

Easy-on-the budget, do-it-yourself projects in the bedroom decorating scheme at left include old dressers rejuvenated with a covering of the same paper used on the walls, sprayed with lacquer and topped with glass, and home-sewn draperies and bedspreads in a crisp floral pattern.

If you keep your eyes open you can find treasures all around you. Below, an old-fashioned washstand was transformed into a record cabinet. The towel rack and the legs were removed, and a box base was added. The facelifting is completed by new hardware, paint, and a top covering.

embark on a budget plan to bring more color into a room. If they're worn out and need replacing, you should consider carefully whether you want to replace them with more vivid things.

Otherwise, brighten up with paint, wallpaper, fabrics, and products of personal skill.

You can cool the scene with blues and greens; warm it up with yellows, oranges, and tints and shades of red.

Rooms that have a sunny exposure take to cooling applications of the receding colors. The blue of the sky and the green of grass promote relaxed, serene feelings. They are always appropriate in a bath, regardless of whether the room has many or few windows or whether they face north or south.

Pattern can coordinate your total decorating theme. The trend toward carrying patterns from one room to another—bedroom and bath, kitchen and eating area, living room and entry hall—is justifiably popular because it creates smooth effects and unifies overall schemes.

Even if you are hesitant to introduce a flamboyant pattern in a much-lived-in room of the home—living room or family room—you needn't pass pattern by. You can use it safely and successfully in dining room or bathrooms that are ordinarily occupied for only brief periods.

Never spurn a spool chest. When the modest secondhand model above was stripped of its old varnish and antiqued in a soft gray-blue it became a charming and useful decorator antique. Insets of yellow caning replaced the missing glass panels of the drawers, giving the chest a cheerful accent.

The inviting eating center at right is the result of do-it-yourself projects. The simply tailored curtains and bright cushions are homemade, and the country-kitchen furniture was bought unpainted and finished at home. Even the floor covering was a home effort—vinyl tiles, easy to set down and keep clean.

How to choose patterns

Next in importance to color for a beginner in decorating is the impact of pattern. Well-chosen pattern can be the most exciting element in your scheme. You will be wise, however, to limit yourself to one pattern in a single room, for it takes a sure eye to combine several pleasingly.

In choosing a pattern that will be given emphasis in a scheme, think scale. A big, bold pattern that would be effective in a large room would dwarf a small one.

Patterns in monotones and in related color schemes (varying shades of one hue, or two or more shades that are neighbors on the color wheel, such as blue and green) are easier for the amateur to work with than those that include many hues and make it harder to decide which will dominate.

You can give a dining room the charm of French country style by refinishing a table and chairs and installing a sideboard and a quaint wine-map poster. The table is antiqued in a brilliant yellow, and the top is given a sea-green tortoiseshell finish. The chair seats are covered with felt. The picturesque open shelves are 1 × 12-inch boards.

Paint and imagination gave this desk a new lease on life. The desk was sanded, the legs were renailed, and the whole was painted with black enamel. Pictures from an old fashion magazine, cut out in paper-doll style, were glued on top to make a collage, then given several coats of clear lacquer.

A pair of sturdy coffee tables were once high-backed chairs that were picked up at a re-sale shop. The backs were cut off, and pieces of travertine marble were cut to size and placed on the seats. (Many new vinyls imitate marble well and could be substituted at much less cost.) The bases were antiqued with white paint and umber, wiped on and off.

If you are considering a bold pattern in a decorating scheme, don't decide on the basis of a small sample. Order a roll of wallpaper or a bolt of cloth (arranging to return it if it won't do). Spread it out in the room and see how you like the pattern when it is used generously. If you don't like it in quantity, maybe it will work as an accent.

To achieve a luxury look on a budget, combine a print with a solid color that perfectly matches a shade in the pattern. Choose a print that is priced within a limit you have established (not overlooking print bed linens) and select one of its colors for contrast.

If you're not sure of your own taste and judgment, study commercial lines of coordinated print and plain papers and fabrics and let them guide your choice.

In choosing the print, keep in mind the size of the room in which it will be featured. Is it rather small? Better stick to the smaller prints. But if the room is of heroic proportions, let yourself go on a bold figure; you can afford to splash it around generously without risk of making the room appear crowded or cramped. Use white or coordinated solid color for a contrast, and your basic scheme is complete.

Tips for young homemakers

For newly married couples and young men and women who are living away from home for the first time, a wealth of material is available to help in decorating and furnishing a home or an apartment. Under appropriate headings in these volumes you will find practical and professional advice on basic carpentry, painting, sewing. Study these carefully *before* you start a decorating project—not later, after you have learned the hard way that there are, indeed, tricks to all trades.

Ask, too, for advice when you shop for materials to use in a home decorating or remodeling project. The sales person may not offer unsolicited advice (after all, you could be an expert), but he or she can probably provide many helpful tips if you explain that you are a beginner. To get the best advice, describe as precisely as possible the particular job you want to do.

Manufacturers of furniture, fabrics, carpets, paint, and wallpaper offer pamphlets that are another fine source of helpful information for beginners. When you are buying any of the myriad products that may enter into your particular project, or any of the tools with which to work, ask whether an instructional pamphlet is available. If it is, study it thoroughly before you begin. It could save you a great deal both in time and money.

Major items should have budget priority for young homemakers. It is wise to spend a generous portion of the furnishings budget on good-quality sofas, mattresses and box springs, and lounge chairs. Such items can be expected to wear well, both in structural parts and in upholstery, and to continue their useful lives as the family moves on to larger and more permanent quarters.

But this is only the beginning of establishing a home that has comfort, warmth, and charm. Loving and careful attention to detail is the special ingredient in decorating that only you can add.

Different styles and periods blend happily when color is used with a lavish hand. Old chairs were rejuvenated with bright paint and covered in softly greenish fabric. The impressive table was made from an old base and a new marble top.

An inviting area took its decorating theme from a patterned wall covering. The picnic table and bench were painted turquoise to match one color in the wallpaper. Notice how a small touch of black in the wrought-iron wall decoration sharpens the effect of the color scheme.

A young girl's dressing table was fashioned from scrap lumber and a mirror for the central section, and fiberboard backing covered with felt for the two side frames. Souvenirs, photographs, and other treasures can be pinned onto the felt surface to give the bedroom an air of originality.

The primitive charm of Pennsylvania Dutch motifs was used here in decorating table, chairs, and wall clock. If you don't want to improvise your own designs, use commercially available stencils and then color the flower and heart shapes.

Add sparkle to an entrance. On a solid-core, flush door, frame in an area with decorative molding. Run three more strips of molding down the door vertically, and paint the panels between in a bright color that best suits the exterior.

Low-cost ideas for children's rooms

To please the younger members of your family, decorate their rooms in ways that make them clearly his or hers alone. It is wise to select basic furniture—such as a bed and a chest of drawers—so that it will be capable of continued use into the teens and beyond.

On the other hand, wallpaper, draperies, bedspreads, and decorative items should reflect the child's age if he is to feel that it's truly "my room."

These elements of decorating can be very inexpensive indeed—so that you won't mind changing the scene every few years—if you supply the labor. Use your child's favorite colors and feature his interests of the moment as you decorate his room; his store of happy memories will be your reward.

Will it have been a saving next year?

Plan for the future as you make your selections now. It would be unsound economy to invest a great deal of money in major items of furnishings if you expect to move to a distant location in the foreseeable future. Draperies and floor coverings purchased for one home are unlikely to fit another; and it is often more expensive to move furniture for a long distance than it would be to replace it. On the other hand, don't postpone decorating plans because of this possibility. Just keep it in mind, so that the major items you buy or make will be versatile enough to fit into another home, and the minor items will be inexpensive enough to discard if moving costs prove prohibitive.

When you purchase furniture for children, remember that they develop quickly. Just a few years will bring rapid changes in size and unpredictable changes in tastes. Today's baby will soon become a child too tall for a crib and too sophisticated for a nursery. Little girls may suddenly turn tomboy and then just as suddenly become sweetly feminine again. Little boys very soon develop strong aversions to baby things.

If you plan later to undertake a remodeling project that will involve adding one or more rooms, try to choose major pieces of furniture that will allow for a shift of placement and that will blend with additional furnishings when the change is made.

This beautiful old walnut bed, found in a secondhand store, is a fine example of a bargain transformed into a useful and decorative item of furniture. The oval section in the headboard was removed and covered with plaid fabric that matches the dust ruffle.

Built-in twin beds allow two tiny tots to share a small bedroom and still have a play area in the center of the room. (For a complete Project Plan, order PP 3408-3.)

Accessories for every pocketbook

Never underestimate the importance of accessories in decorating a room. They play a vital role, offering pleasant clues to the personalities of the owners and making the room as unique as the tastes and interests of the people who live there.

Unfortunately, the inexperienced decorator often fails to realize the value of accessories. He may give them little time or thought, allowing objects to accumulate haphazardly, keeping them for sentimental reasons, or displaying them in a random fashion.

Interesting accessories can make or mar a room scheme. The most carefully arranged and decorated room can be bland and uninteresting if the personalities of its occupants are not reflected in its furnishings. For this reason, accessories deserve as much attention as any other element in room decor. Often they are the most memorable feature of a room, even though they may be the least costly.

In general, accessories are either purely decorative (art objects, antique implements, paintings, and so on) or functional. Functional accessories include lamps, pillows, mirrors, flower containers, room dividers, bowls, and the ubiquitous ash tray. Imagination, inspiration, and good taste must go into the selection of accessories. Sometimes you see an object and know immediately that it's just what you need for a certain spot in your home.

When your budget is tight, it places an additional limitation on your free selection of the "just right" accessory. But that is no reason to give up, to say you can't afford what you want and you won't have anything at all until you're more affluent.

Instead, see what you can do to imitate or duplicate more expensive room accents, using your own labor as money saver.

Study the pages of this encyclopedia and of other books or magazines that concentrate on decorating. Browse through store displays for new ideas. Make mental notes of the accessory ideas you like when you visit.

Poorly placed windows (behind the bed) can be blocked out with a clever combination of wood framing and lavish use of fabric. Pleasantly curving arches of plywood are painted in a shade borrowed from the fabric print.

For a portable wall and lighting installation, this room has two fiberboard screens covered with fabric. Gold-toned wall brackets and tubing were screwed into the wood framing to hold lamp shades. Wiring is concealed behind the screens.

Bold blue felt applied to a wall recess makes a dramatic ceiling-high headboard. The trick works just as well on a flat wall, with neat trim moldings applied at each side of the felt. For adhesive, use white glue, thinned slightly with water.

Custom treatment for inexpensive cocoa-fiber mats puts a note of welcome at your front door. Stencil a design on the mat and spray-paint it with flat enamel. Your monogram or street number, garden posies, a family pet in silhouette—all of these and many more are possible subjects for such use.

Delight one of the younger members of your family with a bed canopy made with strips of felt in hues that harmonize with the total room scheme. The felt strips are 4 inches wide and 8 feet long. They are supported by two painted wooden poles held in place with monofilament line.

We hope here to spark your imagination with accessory ideas you can copy, modify, make, or buy inexpensively to add a personal note to whatever room in your house you find lacking in individuality.

Decorator touches with accessories you have made with a small cash outlay can dress up a room, be a focal point, make it a reflection of your tastes and interests, and increase its beauty and comfort.

Accessories must suit the overall flavor of a room if they are to be effective. Consider the size, shape, color, theme, texture, and purpose of an accessory before you make it or display it in any room of your home. Does it blend harmoniously with the color scheme you have already established?

If your room furnishings are primarily of one period (modern, provincial, American colonial), make sure the accessories keep to the same period or are in harmony with it.

A functional accessory that lends itself well to numerous dramatic treatments is the headboard. Headboards can range all the way from a custom-built version with shelves and

Here is a way to carpet your stairs for as little as $15. Shop for carpet remnants, samples, or small throw rugs in different colors. Try to keep the whole collection in about the same weight, texture, and blend of fibers to assure uniform wearability. Cut all sections to fit, and use tacks to hold each piece securely.

recessed lighting, to an upholstered one, to a simple panel of fabric or wall covering glued to the wall. Whether you are a novice at do-it-yourself projects or a seasoned handyman, you can achieve a professional-looking headboard. It could consist of an arrangement of framed prints or etchings, a panel of fabric that matches the draperies and bedspread and is fastened to the wall and outlined with a narrow wood molding, a wallpaper mural, or a strip of wallpaper that harmonizes with the color scheme and furnishings. An outmoded bedstead of wood could be padded and upholstered.

In choosing a headboard design remember that it must blend with the room's decor and that it must be in scale with the size of the bed. Whether you prefer something massive, something elegant, or something dainty, study your room carefully before you decide.

Well-chosen pictures are a time-honored means of adding beauty and color to the rooms of your home. You can gain even greater impact if you learn the trick of using colored mats tastefully. To obtain the desired effect, first consider the picture itself to decide what color mat would be the most appropriate.

For an unusual wall hanging, frame a piece of fabric. The one pictured below is a Picasso print. The cost of the fabric and materials for the frame was only $5. When you buy a fabric for such a treatment, choose one with a dramatic motif, and then enhance the design with a solid-color fabric matting that picks up a color in the design.

Hobbies and collections produce interesting and colorful accents that can add zest to a bland room. In addition to sparking the decorating theme, they reflect the interests and personalities of the family members. There is only one important rule to follow in order to give them their proper setting: mix formal with formal, and informal with informal. A careless mixture never produces successful results.

If any member of your family is an amateur photographer, painter, or sculptor, or has a hobby that involves collecting, work out a distinctive way to display his or her specialty effectively. Give it an appropriate setting and make it a vital part of the room decor.

Here is a conversation piece of artwork that you can make yourself, whether or not you have creative talent. It consists of two widths of brilliantly patterned wallpaper, pasted to a 48 × 52-inch hardboard and framed with batten strips.

Paint a square—or a rectangle—of plywood or fiberboard to serve as a background. Buy unfinished molding to make the frame. Fasten the frame in place by nailing through the back of the background mounting.

Once you have decided upon the kind of hobby collection you wish to use in a given room, the next consideration is to display it to the best advantage. The method will, of course, depend in part upon what it is you wish to display: the size of the individual objects, the number of objects in the collection, and whether the collection is complete or will be added to from time to time.

Bookshelves and bookcases make perfect display cases for certain kinds of objects. Crystal, porcelain figurines, pieces of pewter, silver, copper, or brass, sculptured objects, rare books, and many other things will show up well on open shelves.

For other objects, a decorative backdrop may be more appropriate. You can make your own backdrop by stretching a piece of colorful fabric across a wall, then fastening it to the surface. Such a fabric panel can be glued or stapled to the wall or, if you want the professional touch, you can use a pressure-sensitive tape that has a high-tack adhesive on both sides. Spread the fabric on the floor and press tape about ¼ inch from the edge on all four sides. Remove the backing from the tape a little at a time as you press the fabric in place

For the family that enjoys Americana, a Franklin stove makes an appealing alternative to a fireplace. A genuine antique like this is costly, but excellent reproductions may be purchased for about $80.

The planter and splashblock above right and the pot-holder or cachepot above left were all made for pennies from easy-to-use concrete. Plastic mixing bowls, wastebaskets, and cardboard boxes, all of graduated sizes, are used as the exterior and interior molds. After they were lined with plastic sheeting, the molds are filled with cement, wrapped in plastic sheeting, and left to dry for three days. The molds lift out undamaged, ready for further use. Colored pots can be made by adding pigment to the dry cement before it is mixed with water.

Handsome planters like the one at left can be made in a few hours from fireplace grates. After lightly sanding the grate, give it a new coat of paint, then fill it with potted plants. This unusual planter is fairly portable, and can be moved around the patio wherever an empty spot needs to be brightened. The plants can be varied with the seasons.

The versatile mobile planter at right rolls around your patio or house on casters ▶ and can be built easily with inexpensive lumber. The best waterproofing is a tin liner, but plastic sheeting can be used. The box is painted, then filled with pebbles or marble chips to which water can be added for humidity; potted plants are then set on this surface.

on the wall. If and when the time comes that you want a change, simply pull the tape slowly and gently from the wall to remove the panel.

A fabric background can be used for showing off a collection of photographs, posters, or art reproductions, in frames or merely matted. Informal burlap or monk's cloth is well suited to family rooms and children's rooms, or you might repeat a fabric used in upholstery or drapery as a coordinating touch.

For collections of shells, flat silver, demitasse cups, paperweights, or mounted butterflies, you might consider converting an old coffee table into a showcase.

Replace the top of the coffee table with a wood-framed glass top that lets you look down into the display box. For greater showmanship, you could install concealed lighting beneath the frame. Whatever collection you are displaying, arrange it in an interesting fashion.

Wall-hung shadow boxes, which you can buy or make yourself, offer another dramatic way to display the kinds of room accents that have been suggested here. Velvet lining in colors coordinated with the room scheme could make these elegant and unusual.

A collection of gorgeously colored mounted butterflies makes an unusually effective wall grouping. So do four or five Japanese fans in shades that harmonize with other room colors.

Pottery—of your own design if you're a potter, or a few unusual pieces purchased with your decorating plans in mind—offers still another ingenious method of introducing small but important amounts of the colors you'll use as a means of enlivening a room.

The family room, geared to casual living, is usually an appropriate place to display less formal accessories, such as pop posters. This is one room in which family interests and talents

can provide the most interesting of decorative accents. Sports trophies, music scores, menu covers, record album jackets—any of these, and many more, can be incorporated into the family room decor. You need only take a fresh look at all the things your family has collected to discover a world of possibilities.

If you are a home gardener, or simply one who appreciates growing things, bring the natural richness and variety of plants and flowers into your home. The decorative uses of live plants are nearly endless, and in most cases inexpensive as well. Flowering house plants, annuals dug while in bloom and set into pots, planters with ivy or philodendron—all add depth and texture to bare surfaces, just as cut flowers and greenery lend the special brightness of their short lives.

Capitalize on plants as an element in your decorating scheme by grouping them in a dramatic fashion. One plant, unless it is very large, may make little difference in adding visual appeal to a room; nor will a few plants monotonously lined up on a window sill add much interest. But five or six plants together in an unusual combination will catch the eye and become an important feature. Massing plants on a stepladder, for example, or in an antique highchair or wheelbarrow can give solidity and texture to a hard-to-fill corner. An old-fashioned sled or child's wagon, dusted off and waxed, makes an ideal display piece for potted plants, as does a dome-shaped birdcage hung in a prominent spot.

If you are uncertain about the light and water requirements of house plants, acquaint

You can contrive an unusual decorator-piece planter by stacking flower pots. To keep your pyramid of pots from collapsing, fasten the rims together with epoxy glue. Those pictured at left are 10-inch azalea pots. You can make yours larger or smaller to fit your needs. In a more spacious setting, use three or four pot columns of different sizes, with each one displaying a different kind of plant.

You can use flowering or foliage plants, or a combination of the two. During summer months, grow some of your favorite annuals and perennials in these large pots.

yourself with their needs. (See *House Plants, Vol. 10.*) Most plants require a certain amount of care and light, but there are some undemanding varieties that are perfect candidates for dusky corners and empty walls.

For the youngsters of the family, you can foster an interest in nature by establishing a terrarium with small varieties of growing plants. A terrarium—from the Latin *terra,* meaning earth—is a glass-walled little world of nature that you can construct, experiment with, change, and study in your own home.

An old fish tank that you might find at a thrift shop makes an ideal container for a terrarium. If there is no cover, you can have a piece of glass cut to the proper size to serve as a lid and to keep a constant level of moisture in the terrarium. If you're not an authority on plants, ask your greenhouse man or florist to

The wall-hung lavabo is a natural and appropriate accessory for rooms that turn to the provincial—French, Spanish, or Italian—for decorating inspiration. It provides an ideal container for an arrangement of flowers and greenery. When the lavabo is hung on a solid-colored wall, as in the photo, it takes on greater importance if it is mounted on a slab of wood cut to follow the generally curving outline. The wood mounting can be given a finish that dramatizes the lavabo and harmonizes with furniture woods.

The personalized planter-end table can be built in any size to fit your living room or family room. Make the basic box from ¾-inch fir plywood, and set it on short, square wooden legs. Cut out a piece of the top for the planter section and build in a small box to hold the earth and gravel. Use a metal or plastic dishpan liner in this box. Give the entire unit a painted finish, or cover it with plastic laminate. For a traditional or country theme, use round or carved legs. Decorative hardware trim can be in whatever style best suits the decor of your room.

help you choose plants to include; they must be varieties that thrive on high humidity. Place your terrarium where it will receive good light and watch it grow.

While all these suggestions are fresh in your mind, why don't you start a thorough search of closets, cupboards, and drawers. You may unearth many items that should take their place as decorative accessories, along with the hobby and collection items.

Most of the things you will find can probably be displayed as is. Others may need a little touching up or transforming.

You can build this bookish window treatment that frames a view and also provides storage space. Construct the shelf unit of four vertical 8-foot 1 × 12s, and divide the space horizontally as desired.

An attic room is turned into a retreat for boys. Brick-patterned vinyl paper covers the wall; shutters and a canopy dress up the window. Red floor tiles form a hearth for the fake fireplace. The lamppost and corral fence add decorative touches.

Arches that add window drama are constructed of ¾-inch plywood secured to the tops of four standard lumber verticals. Cover the inner edges of the verticals and arches with a 3-inch strip of ¼-inch plywood. Paint or stain the unit and add café curtains.

In the room at right, window panels were made from a 2¾- ▶ yard split length of 48-inch material. Each panel was hung from a top pole and weighted at floor level with another pole run through the bottom casing.

Cost-cutting ideas for your windows

Various types of windows require different treatments. Before you decide whether you will use curtains, draperies, shutters, blinds, or a combination of two or more, study your room carefully. How much light do you want to admit? Do you want to blot out an uninteresting view, or do you want the window to frame a picturesque scene?

If you decide to use draperies and/or curtains, you can save money by making them yourself. If you buy them, you can save by choosing stock sizes rather than the more expensive custom-made styles. If the length is

This decorative installation consists of strips of braid stretched on wooden café poles mounted at top and bottom of the window. The strips can be sewn to fit the size of the pole or tacked onto the pole.

Add interest to a standard window by cutting a plywood arch and fitting it into the top of the window. Paint the arch and the mullions black. Antique some unfinished shutter panels, along with the window trim. Use colorful fabric in the shutters.

not right, you can shorten or lengthen them accordingly.

Window shades offer a great opportunity to add to your decorative effect. You can buy stock shades in white or colors, and trim them yourself. Use braid or fringe that accents your room furnishings, or appliquéd designs or borders of fabric that is used elsewhere in the room. Add shade pulls of your own design; these could be large plastic or brass rings, tassels, or pompoms made of yarn. A matching valance made of shade cloth and mounted on a curtain rod can give the same effect as an expensive custom-made cornice.

A cantilevered bench and matching wall liven up a living room or family room. Build an 18-inch-deep bench frame of 2 × 4s and fasten it to the wall studs with lag screws. Apply inexpensive grooved plywood to the wall and bench, using either nails or glue. Then paint your handiwork.

If this room appeals to you, and your decorating budget is limited, use prepasted wallpaper that you can hang yourself. Many such papers have matching fabrics that can be used as trim or to make bedspreads, draperies, or cushions.

Every mother who alters her children's clothing also enjoys putting her sewing talent to work in an artistic way.

In the photo, ordinary bedroom and bathroom linens have been personalized with gay flower trims appliquéd on towels, sheets, and pillowcases.

Saving through sewing

Needlework, whether it pertains to useful or purely decorative items, can be a means of providing accents that are charming as well as easy on the budget. It is also an excellent way to put the imprint of yourself on the furnishings of a room.

In addition to the useful items that immediately come to mind such as draperies, curtains, bedspreads, and slipcovers (see *Draperies,* Vol. 7; *Bedding and Bed Linens,* Vol. 3; *Slipcovers,* Vol. 16; *Upholstery,* Vol. 17 for complete how-to-do-it instructions), there is an almost endless list of needlework projects.

Your choice of project will depend largely on your skills and interests, your decorating needs and personal preferences, and the amount of time and money you are willing to spend on the project. Take your pick from wall hangings; needlepoint covers for chair seats and footstools; woven, crocheted, hooked, or braided rugs; cushions or pillows that are pieced, quilted, or embroidered; knitted or crocheted afghans; appliqué designs for slipcovers, lamp shades, window shades; and table linens.

Visit knitting shops and the needlework sections of department stores to see the array of materials available for needlework projects. Many items come in kit form, packaged with all materials needed to complete the project and easy-to-follow instructions. Many needlework departments have trained personnel to advise and instruct customers in stitchery and crafts. (See *Crafts,* Vol. 6; *Framing and Matting,* Vol. 8; *Hooked Rugs,* Vol. 10; *Pillows,* Vol. 14.)

To make an attractive entryway rug like the one above at a very nominal cost, buy discontinued rug samples for about fifty cents each. Dye the samples first, then cut them into desired shapes and glue them to burlap backing.

A decorator hammock and stand for sunning or stargazing is easy to make. All you need is 3 yards of 36-inch canvas and colorful cotton material for an appliqué. Improvise your own design—the wilder the better—and sew it onto the canvas.

The photo shows how a porch can be shaded with only a modest expenditure. Large screw eyes were placed on the railing and at the top, to hold the canvas securely in place. Wooden dowels pass through hems in the canvas.

A good place to begin

Outdoor decorating projects can be every bit as effective as those geared to the living rooms of your home. The men of the family should be easy to involve in such projects, since they often involve carpentry skills that a man understands and likes.

Sturdy, colorful tables, benches, and chairs for a porch or patio require less finesse in construction and painting than do pieces intended for interior use. Starting with outdoor pieces, therefore, makes good sense for the do-it-yourself beginner.

The smaller cost involved is an important factor for the beginner, too. A lower grade of lumber is usually acceptable in construction of porch and patio furniture. This automatically reduces the money investment in the project and thus gives the beginner less to worry about; he can embark on the process of learning without having to fear that his inexperience may lead to costly errors.

Flue tile, a surprisingly versatile and sturdy material, was put to a distinctive use in the patio table at far left. Heavy enough not to tilt, the tile is 20 inches square and 2 feet in length. The tabletop is constructed from ten 3-foot 2 × 4s and held together with two angle irons to form a frame that fits snugly over the table's base.

Looking a little like an earthbound meteorite, the egg-shaped planter on the fence is made of volcanic rock, lightweight and easy to work. Any sharp tool can be used to scoop out planting pockets.

Four freestanding wooden planters add drama to this patio but can be used as separate units. All are made of 2 × 2-inch boards. The low box measures 2 × 2 feet; the verticals are 4, 4½, and 5 feet high.

The suspended planter at upper right is made of two circles of exterior-grade plywood, 18 inches in diameter. Cut a hole in the upper board to hold a 14-inch pot, lace a sash chain through screw eyes to make a drum design, and determine the hanging length of the chains to suit the location. Remember that hanging plants require more frequent watering than plants in the ground.

This space-saving folding bench is 30 inches long, 16 inches deep, and 18 inches high when unfolded. Plate hinges secure the bench to a 6-foot 2 × 4 attached to the wall. The top and banding are made of 1 × 4s. The bench legs, which fold flat against the bench top, are of exterior-grade plywood with 13-inch cutouts.

Ordinary drainage tiles were used to make the garden night lights at lower right. The tiles are 12 inches long and 4 inches wide. Each T-end tile is filled to its opening with gravel, and a votive candle is set in place. Six or seven lights can be made for under $3.

Handyman projects

Dollar-wise decorating produces the best results when you can supply at least part of the necessary labor yourself. Skilled painters and paperhangers receive high hourly rates of pay, and many are unwilling to take on small jobs. Professional upholsterers and makers of draperies and slipcovers are also highly paid.

If you can become proficient in one or more of these skills, you will be able to stretch your decorating dollars a great deal further. You will also gain the extra reward that accompanies doing a job yourself—the satisfaction of turning out a professional-looking product.

The school systems in many cities offer adult education courses both for the beginner and the more advanced do-it-yourselfer. Courses that are frequently available teach the basic skills involved in upholstery, drapery making, furniture refinishing, cabinetmaking, caning, and weaving, to name only a few.

Patio lights made from flower pots require one standard pot and one azalea pot each. Carefully break out the bottom of the pot used for the lower section. Enlarge surfaces for joining together by filing pot rims. Using a carbide-pointed bit, drill holes in the sides of the pots. Notch the sides of the drainage hole in the top pot to receive loops of chain. Weave waterproof electrical wire into the chain and work it through the notched hole. Turn the chain at right angles to notches of pot to secure. Plug the light into an outdoor electric socket. Use a low-wattage bulb.

Here, in very limited space, a refreshing sight to all who enter is created by an ornate bird cage, a discarded window given a tissue-paper "painting," and fresh green ferns.

To work a tissue design on glass, cut a pattern from paper of one color, place it against the glass (in horizontal position), and shellac. Repeat in layers of related or contrasting shades until you get the final effect you desire.

Many other skills you can learn yourself with the aid of a textbook written for the do-it-yourself amateur. Sometimes you may be able to enlist the aid of a relative or friend who is proficient in such projects to help you with your first attempt and reveal some of the "tricks of the trade."

Compare the investment in a few tools such as an adaptable electric drill, a saw, a hammer, screwdrivers, chisels, and planes with the hourly rates of professional carpenters in your area. Nationwide, they are high, and they seem to be rising all the time. To save you time and money, most hardware stores have reasonable rental fees for power equipment.

How to economize on lighting

If you have spent time and thought selecting and matching colors to make your home more beautiful, use the same care in selecting the proper lighting fixtures and lamps.

Lighting fixtures are available in styles to suit any type of furnishings. They are classified as ceiling mountings, movable lamps, and wall lights. If you must economize on lighting fixtures, choose inexpensive ones for the bedrooms, which draw the least attention. If you can splurge on only one, let it be the dining area fixture, or a dramatic one for the entryway.

If you have old table lamps or bridge or floor lamps, consider rejuvenating them to do away with their shabby or outdated appearance.

Pottery lamp bases can be painted or antiqued; metal bases can be cleaned, polished, and lacquered. If table lamps are too low, you can fasten a pottery, wood, or metal addition to the bottom with epoxy glue; or you can replace the harp with a taller one. Lamp shades adapt well to ornamentation that harmonizes with other furnishings. Trim them with braid, fringe, or appliqué designs; or cover the entire shade with fabric or wallpaper that is used elsewhere in the room.

Glamorize an inexpensive porch lamp by covering it with squares of colored glass that will glow with color when the light is turned on. Attach the squares with transparent, glass-to-glass-bonding cement, and fill in the spaces with grout. Experiment with light bulbs of various wattages to find the one that shows off the colors to best advantage.

The novel hanging fixture below starts with four pieces of white plastic ⅛ inch thick and measuring 9 × 12½ inches, plus a top section 9 inches square. The sections are butted together and glued. A hole is drilled for the cord, and four cork "hot mats" are glued over the plastic frame for an interesting decorative effect.

This useful bed frame is designed for a small bedroom and a small budget. Because the bunk has simple lines, and because it can be repainted from time to time to suit a changing color scheme, it will keep up-to-date with a youngster from the time he first graduates from the crib to an adult bed straight through to college. With a little carpentry skill, you can build the whole unit easily from inexpensive lumber. The joints are of simple construction, and the pieces are just a series of rectangles. For more ideas about compact beds, see *Bunks*, p. 670.

Beds you can build

If you have a capable and willing handyman around the house, building a bed such as the one pictured here is not too difficult a project. (For complete instructions, order Project Plan 3607-9.) If you plan to give the bed a painted finish, you can build it from inexpensive lumber.

To start with a simpler version, you could build just a wooden frame to hold the box spring and mattress, and hang bookshelves on the wall above it.

If you have a wooden bedstead of ancient vintage that you would like to use, you can shorten the legs, or cut down the headboard and/or footboard. For a contemporary touch, upholster the headboard with a leatherlike material; for a traditional or country effect, use a fabric that matches or accents the bedspread. The finish you choose will depend on other furnishings in the room. It could be a painted, antiqued, or natural wood finish.

An old brass bedstead, even though tarnished, can be restored to take a position of prominence in the room; it can be cleaned, buffed, and given a coat of clear lacquer. Wicker bedsteads are inexpensive; they are attractive in the natural finish, or they can be spray-painted in a lively color that complements the room furnishings.

Make your own room dividers

Two separate atmospheres can be created in one area of space through the use of room dividers. Dividers can range from a permanent installation built of expensive materials to inexpensive ones that can be moved as the space requirements of the family change.

A divider can extend from ceiling to floor to make a room into completely separate areas, or it can be of cabinet height merely to indicate a separation of activities. If you want a divider that does not shut out light or reduce air circulation, choose one with an openwork design.

Materials are available for every type of divider. Some you may be able to salvage from buildings that are being demolished; others you may have to purchase from a building supply dealer.

Materials you might find at building demolition sites include shutters, turned wood poles, and wrought-iron gates or fencing. Louvered shutters can be painted or stained and installed as permanent dividers, or hinged to act as a screen divider. Turned wood poles, uniformly spaced and attached to supports at top and bottom, divide space without blocking view. An iron gate or section of iron fencing can be hung above a storage cabinet or bookshelves. Wrought iron fits in equally well with Mediterranean or contemporary furnishings.

A folding screen with solid panels can function as a room divider and be moved from room to room as space requirements indicate. The panels can be covered with wallpaper, fabric, or a collection of menu covers or theater programs. If someone in your family is creative, use original art on the panels of the folding screen.

Fabric panels hung from a ceiling track offer many decorative opportunities. The fabric can be felt, damask, or other type of drapery material, or a sheer fabric that allows air to circulate and light to filter through. To

This see-through room divider requires three yards of semi-sheer printed fabric; the result is a translucent screen that subtly veils the view but does not entirely block it out. The fabric is hemmed on all four sides, and a lattice molding is inserted at top and bottom.

For these thick-and-thin swinging doors you will need knot-free, 1-inch lumber. The planks should be ripped into strips slightly wider than they are thick. Glue the planks together, alternating the wide and narrow edges. Use heavy-duty hinges such as the double-action pivot type.

Have you already guessed that the striking room divider pictured above is really an assemblage of terra-cotta flower pots, held secure by dowels run through the drainage holes? The twin chests are painted an exactly matching red.

Potted plants in a metal-lined tray complete the picture. A handsome wrought-iron candelabrum attached to the wall helps to further the primitive Mexican flavor of the clay-pot construction, which resembles lathe-turned columns.

The single unit shown above includes a desk, a bookcase, and an entry divider. This space-saving unit can be built by the home handyman. The unit can be painted or given a natural wood finish, according to your preference. It has the appearance of a permanent built-in, but it can be moved with ease. (For a complete Project Plan, order PP 3404-2.)

Lengths of ball fringe form a room divider in the informal kitchen-family room at right. Buy fringe that is strung on fiber thread and attach it to small strips of wood. This red, white, and blue divider, 4 × 8 feet, cost only $25.

A divider like this one would represent a sizable investment if you were to buy it, but you can construct it yourself with a minimum of tools and at a fraction of its ready-made cost. Make four 18 × 90-inch frames of ¾-inch lumber. Attach strips of woven-wood shade material (available at a shade shop or department store) with half-round molding. Join the finished panels with double-acting hinges. For a stylish finish, add decorative wooden finials.

make the panel hang straight, weight it at the bottom by running brass rods through the hem. For an unusual divider, install a track at both ceiling and floor, and string yarn closely spaced from top to bottom. The yarn could be either of one color or a combination of colors. To add interest, hang a few strings of beads uniformly spaced between the strands of yarn.

Divider frameworks supported by suspension poles can be bought from a building supply dealer. They are inexpensive, easy to install, and movable. Wood filigree and glass panels may be had in a number of patterns to fit these frames. Wood panels and framework can be painted to suit any decor. You might add a touch of individuality by creating panels of your own design.

For a contemporary room, you could build a wood frame that extends from ceiling to

For an unusual and individual treatment, camouflage a wooden cube with a montage of photographs clipped from magazines. This 24-inch cube was constructed of ½-inch plywood. Photograph clippings were glued onto the top and sides, allowed to dry completely (a minimum of 24 hours), and then given a few coats of clear sealer. A final coat of high-gloss varnish made it mar-resistant and a safe resting place for glasses and cups when refreshments are served.

The good-looking patio table at right has a second function: it stores bench and chair cushions neatly under its protective top when they are not in use. The table is made of a 3-foot-square piece of exterior-grade plywood, set firmly on 2-inch-square, 18-inch-high legs placed 18 inches apart. The plywood cushion shelf acts as a low brace between the legs. The top is covered with 6-inch-square quarry tiles that can take all kinds of weather and rough use. The tiles are secured to the plywood with mastic, and grout between them seals the surface. The table is painted with exterior enamel.

floor, and install glass shelves. Plants, small pieces of sculpture, and glass objects placed on such shelves seem almost to be suspended in space. Another suggestion for a contemporary room divider is to use panels of clear and smoke-colored plastic resting on slotted strips of wood, with shelves also of plastic that strengthen the vertical supports and provide a display area.

For a permanent room divider, you might install an accordion wood screen or plastic accordion walls that can be closed to separate space or opened to join two areas. These are especially suited to children's rooms, when complete privacy is desirable at night, and an open area for play is needed during the day.

A planter can be an interesting and decorative divider. Build a boxlike structure of cabinet-base height, about 10 inches deep, and whatever length best suits your room. Make a recessed shelf to fit into the divider about 6 inches below the top. Line the recessed area with waterproof material, place it in the divider, and add plants. For added drama, install a recessed ceiling light to cast its glow onto the plants.

Tables tailored to your needs

Every home needs various types of tables, both functional and decorative. They can also be budget items if you build them yourself, or if you rejuvenate outdated castoffs.

If you explore resale shops, auctions, and house sales, you may find sturdy tables that need only refinishing. If the top is scarred beyond repair, you can add a wood-grain formica or marble top cut to size and attached securely with adhesive. To convert a standard table into a coffee or cocktail table, cut the legs so that the overall height is 16½ inches.

For a coffee or cocktail table with a sleek contemporary look, make a frame of ¾-inch-square aluminum tubing, which can be cut with a hacksaw. Tap the corner joints together with a mallet. For the top, use a piece of slate cut from a blackboard, sealed with finishing oil and laid rough side up.

Inexpensive tables for the patio, terrace, or porch can be made from precast concrete blocks. Choose blocks with patterned perforations for the legs, and top with cap blocks.

If you should fall heir to an old round oak dining table with a heavy pedestal base, you can use it in several different ways. If you want to use it as a dining table, but feel it is too massive, replace the pedestal base with four slender, tapered legs. If you want to use it as a coffee table, and your room allows for one of this size, cut down the pedestal to coffee-table height. For a game table for the family room, cover the top with green felt and achieve a professional gaming-table atmosphere. For patio or poolside use, drill a hole in the center and insert a colorful lawn umbrella; lacquer the table to match. Such a round table can also be separated into two halves and used as serving or console tables.

A peninsula desk for a couple of boys adds a splash of warm coral to a cream-turquoise color scheme. The sturdy divider-desk provides study facilities and peace-keeping separation. Needed are two unpainted chests, ¾-inch plywood, and wood-grained laminated plastic. Cut the plywood and nail it together in an L shape, adding aprons. The dimensions may vary according to the height of the chests, but allow about 25 inches for knee room. Bond the plastic to the wood surfaces. Do a workmanlike job of assembling the parts by installing the screws through the undersides of the desk top.

A corner table like this one turns twin beds into a seating arrangement by day. Carefully measure the width and height of your beds; plan the size of the table so that one bed will slide under it smoothly. Cut two squares (about 3 × 3 feet) of ¾-inch fir plywood. Then cut two full-length sides about 10 inches wide for the back and two shorter sides to form the back of the exposed bookshelf. Glue and nail these six pieces together, and apply wood veneer tape to the edges.

Consider the cube and its infinite decorative potential. Buy an unfinished wooden box—or make one yourself. Then transform it with tricks like those pictured and described here.

To copy the box at left, which measures 19 × 18 inches, use iron-on plastic laminate. First cut pieces of laminate to fit the six sides of the cube. Separate a piece from its backing.

Set an electric iron for heat appropriate to cotton fabric and apply to a small area of the laminate, pressing for about 25 seconds; then proceed until you have "ironed on" the whole piece. Immediately, using a damp cloth, wipe and apply pressure to cool the adhesive so that it sets. Cover the remaining sides of the cube in the same way.

A tremendous variety of patterns is now available in plastic laminates. The one shown is a wood grain, but solid colors and patterns of many kinds can also be had.

Set a pair of cubes in front of a living-room sofa to act as coffee tables; or place one at each end of the sofa to serve as end tables.

Pressure-sensitive wallpaper—that is, paper with adhesive backing—is used to create a finish for this cube. Shown here is a contemporary black-and-white striped pattern, but many designs are available in this group of papers. To duplicate the effect of this cube, prepare an 18 × 18-inch wooden cube by giving it a coat of shellac. Next cut striped wallpaper into 6 × 6-inch squares. (It will take nine squares to cover each of the cube's six surfaces.) Apply the squares in an alternating pattern to get the effect shown. For added durability, apply several coats of clear sealer and a final coat of high-gloss finish.

Ordinary wallpaper may also be used in this fashion, but it must be glued in place and allowed to dry very thoroughly before applying the coats of sealer. Such a cube is a clever way to unify a room scheme that features a dramatic wallpaper pattern.

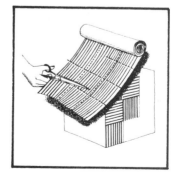

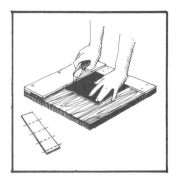

A cube can even be made into a chess- or checkerboard. Apply black-and-white vinyl floor tile to the four sides in alternating fashion. For the top, cut the black and white tiles into two-inch squares (for uniformity, use a jigsaw). All of the tile can be applied to the wooden cube with floor-tile adhesive for a durable bond.

With a little ingenuity, other game patterns such as backgammon could be cut from tiles and applied. An amusing alternative would be the pattern for a ouija board.

If games are not your thing, how about a top that's a collage? It could be created from pictures clipped from magazines, seed catalogs, mail-order catalogs, old books—or whatever strikes your fancy. Glue the parts of your assemblage in place, and let it dry for 24 hours. Then give it a durable surface by applying several coats of sealer plus a finishing coat of glossy plastic varnish to make it moisture- and mar-resistant. The collage treatment could, in fact, be used on all sides of the cube to appeal to the "mod" set.

Covered with tiny gleaming mirrors, a cube might become the sparkling highlight for a room scheme. The mirrors are available in handy 16 × 18-inch sheets and are easy to apply with a special mastic. For a professional-looking finish, apply a stainless-steel rim around the top edges. Miter the corners and apply steel rim with epoxy in the manner shown in the sketch below.

An attractive alternative would be minuscule mosaic tile (either ceramic or plastic), which can be purchased in hobby shops. It could be applied in solid colors, in a design you create yourself, or in one adapted from an old mosaic pattern such as those used by the Romans on floors of their homes.

Art books from the library will contain photographs of these antique mosaic designs which you can modify to suit the amount of space you want to cover. If you attempt this, it will be best to make a pattern on brown paper before you begin.

Bookshelves to build

Assuming that you have a handyman in your home who is adept at basic carpentry, the building and installation of bookshelves is a worthwhile project. In addition to providing easily accessible storage for books, they are an effective display area for decorative accessories and art objects that add warmth and personality to a room.

Depending on your situation—whether your home is a permanent one, or you anticipate a move—decide first just how much money, time, and effort you want to invest. Do you want bookshelves that will be a stationary built-in, or shelves that can be rearranged or moved? When these questions have been resolved, it is time for construction to begin.

If your workshop affords only a minimum of carpentry tools, it will save time and effort to have shelving precut to your measurements at the lumberyard. If you plan to use vertical supports, these can be precut at the same time. Remember that books are heavy, and

Help yourself to this low-cost idea for filling one wall of a living room with an interesting and practical arrangement of shelves to hold books, tape recorder, art objects, and so on.

The basic idea is boxes, boxes, and more boxes! Stacked, wall-hung, bunched—even repeated in squared dimensional paper on wall and ceiling. With you supplying the elbow-grease, this project should cost you less than $100. (Prices of lumber, paper, paint and so on may vary in different areas, so check it out where you live before you begin construction.)

Construct boxes of four pieces of 27 × 14-inch plywood. Vary the size to suit size of squares in your wallpaper, if you intend to copy our idea closely. Attach with glue and finishing nails. Nail heads should be counter-set, filled, and sanded.

Use the same method to attach the backs and divider shelves. Place dividers lengthwise, upright, or in quarters for books, magazines, records, and so on. Line backs of boxes with squares of wallpaper or with blue felt glued in place. Price mentioned should cover the cost of nine boxes, paint, wallpaper, and felt. (For a complete Project Plan, order PP 3510-1.)

The coffee table, end table, and chair shown here are good examples of "finds" one can sometimes make in secondhand and thrift shops, then paint or cover in hues to suit a color scheme. Lamp bases for which new shades can be made or bought are another good item to watch for on bargain hunts.

Look, too, for interesting bric-a-brac, picture frames, and old pieces of china or glassware that will reinforce your decorating scheme.

The storage wall at right, built into a family room, consists mainly of a wall of boxes. Start with a base of 1 × 2 lumber, then build as many as you need of the 7-foot-high boxes 30 inches wide. Drill holes for shelf supports every inch on the inside. Paint the boxes, set them in place, and anchor the tops to the wall. The shelves can be positioned to hold a variety of sizes of books and accessories. The shelves that hold books are of wood, sturdy enough to hold heavy volumes; shelves for accessories are of glass, which gives visual impact to precious items displayed on them. Units of this type can be built in any size. This one was built for $65, only a fraction of the price of a similar ready-made one.

A ladder headboard with storage space to spare was built for only $31. As shown in the photo below, the basic unit consists of four ladders with 1 × 2 pine shelves. Construct vertical pieces of 1 × 3s and insert 1-inch dowels into predrilled holes. To increase the storage capacity, add more shelves. Finish the top section of the headboard with redwood lath. A built-in such as this, in a room shared by two boys, provides an ideal spot for displaying hobby and collection items. The quilted coverlets extending over dust ruffles and the Boston rocker in the foreground provide a quaint and homelike atmosphere, and the replica of a clipper ship is reminiscent of long-gone days.

the shelves must be substantial to bear the weight. For maximum adjustability of the shelves, use metal strips to hold shelf brackets, rather than vertical supports of wood. The metal strips have slots spaced at frequent intervals into which you can fit brackets and space the shelves to suit your needs. The distance between shelves should be at least 1½ inches more than the height of the books.

Bookshelves can be attached directly to the wall, rather than to a set of vertical supports. Numerous shelf bracket designs are available in a variety of wood finishes to harmonize with any furniture style. Metal brackets of either brass or black wrought iron are designed to suit country styles, and others are appropriate in contemporary decorating schemes. All styles and finishes come in several sizes. For adequate support, they should be spaced between 24 and 30 inches apart. Be sure to find out whether your walls are of plaster, drywall, or wallboard before installing brackets. Each type of wall requires a different fastener; be sure to use the right one.

Freestanding bookshelves can be attached to wooden suspension poles that extend from floor to ceiling, or to 1 × 10-inch plywood uprights of room height. Poles with turned designs accent furnishings of traditional or country styles; unadorned poles enhance contemporary furnishings. Freestanding bookshelves are easily moved, removed, or rearranged.

For a completely mobile bookshelf arrangement that can fit any wall size and any room height, use wooden boxes of different sizes in an arrangement that pleases you. Paint them all one color or, for a playroom or family room, paint each one a different vivid color.

The most economical bookcase for those on tight budgets can be made from simple planks and stacked bricks or cinder blocks. Boards of different lengths, stained or painted, can be attractively arranged on bricks piled to accommodate any size book or accessory. For interest, bricks can be covered with fabric.

See *Bookshelves and Bookcases,* Vol. 3; and p. 579, Vol. 4.

The finishing touch

For out-of-date or new unfinished pieces of furniture the following small touches can add up to big effects in home decorating. They can supply the sparkle and liveliness needed to give a drab room a newly imaginative air. And their effectiveness bears little relation to their low cost.

Refinishing drab and uninteresting pieces of furniture with antiquing kits is quick, simple, and most effective. To refresh any piece of outdated furniture the procedure is simple. Wipe the entire surface first with liquid sander, then apply one or two coats of undercoat paint. When this is thoroughly dry, brush on the glazing liquid. Finally, wipe the liquid glaze until you achieve the result you want. Complete instructions, along with all the materials you will need, are included in each antiquing kit.

A wall-wide sweep of shelves and lights presents an airy, graceful effect. This is a wonderful setting for books and a display of beautiful accessories. All but a few of the shelves are adjustable; some are wood, and some are glass. (For a complete Project Plan, order PP 3310-2.)

The large built-in display unit below fills the entire recessed area of one wall. It is constructed mainly of ¾-inch plywood, with ash quarter-round molding bent to conform to the arches. Plastic panels and rosettes across the bottom are nailed and glued on. The entire unit was finished with antiquing glaze.

All necessary items except for the liquid sander are available in kit form, or they may be purchased individually. A wide choice of colors is available, ranging all the way from delicate pastels to beautiful and realistic simulations of wood grains. Check the examples in this section of the antiquing way to rejuvenate furniture. (See *Antiquing,* Vol. 2.)

With painted or lacquered furniture, you can capitalize on color and save in decorating costs at the same time. Start by shopping for unpainted furniture in some of the contemporary or country styles that are on the market. Furniture stores, building supply dealers, department stores, and some paint stores carry extensive lines of unfinished furniture.

Children's art, bright with uninhibited color, interesting in its freedom of expression, deserves more than the cursory inspection it receives when it is brought home from school. You can have a constantly changing art gallery like the one below by attaching wooden frames to cabinets of the kitchen or laundry room. Leave one side of each frame open so that pictures can be slipped in and out for frequent changes of scene. Children will be flattered by presentation of their work.

You may decide to use paint as a rejuvenator for pieces you already own or can buy inexpensively from a thrift or resale shop. Choose paint in colors to suit your decorating scheme. Colors can match, complement, or contrast with others in the room. Your choice will depend on whether you want the piece to blend into the background or to stand out as a sharp accent.

If you lack confidence in your ability to combine colors skillfully, you can purchase a small amount of a printed fabric that contains all the hues you prefer. Then select colors within the print and have them exactly matched at a paint store where paints are mixed to order. This will give you assurance that the colors you combine are harmonious, since printed fabrics of good quality have been designed by artists who are skilled in the use of color.

If you want a quick change of scene that will not strain the budget, put a new color on the walls. Try painting one whole wall (preferably one not broken by doors and windows) in a brilliant shade. When you are seeking a fast, inexpensive way to alter the mood of a room, you will find paint is the cheapest, by far, of any factor in your decorating scheme. (See *Paints and Painting,* Vol. 13.)

If you plan to restore and refinish antiques or other furniture pieces in a wood finish, the first step is to remove all the old finish, wax, and dirt; next comes sanding, first with a coarse grade, and finishing with a fine sandpaper. At this point, you may need to do some gluing or make minor repairs if the piece is weak or wobbly. Inspect the legs and arms of chairs, the drawers of chests and dressers, the doors of cabinets. If they are in need of repair, the time to do it is before the finishing. The finishing treatment will depend on the type of wood involved and whether you want a dull, satin, or glossy finish. (See *Finishes and Refinishing,* Vol. 8.)

Oriental prints have been mounted on the sliding cabinet doors for an interesting decoration. A collection of menus or favorite recipes could be displayed in the same manner. Hinges like those used in stamp albums hold prints on laminated plastic sheets. Clear plastic covers the prints; **two-piece hollow rivets** fasten sheets to doors.

Pink, orange, and purple matchstick panels add an Oriental flavor to a white-walled kitchen. Cut panels into desired sizes and fit them to wooden frames. Hinge the frames at top and bottom.

Used to screen an unlovely view, matchstick bamboo panels still let in filtered light.

Turn a small closet into a canned-goods dispenser and have all your staples in view as soon as you open the door. All it takes is plywood shelves set at an angle, plus facing strips of 1 × 2s to hold the cans steady. When you remove the front can, the one behind it rolls into place in the front row. This type of installation provides a vast amount of easily accessible storage space; the entire unit can be built for about $22.

A complete utensil storage unit like this one can be built for about $26. Just a few hours of handyman ingenuity will unclutter your kitchen. This tall cabinet was revamped with a sheet of perforated plywood fastened to the back wall. Then three plywood shelves were installed, and some vertical divider panels of hardboard to hold baking pans. Hooks can be placed in an arrangement suitable for any collection of pots and pans.

Storage organization can save you money

Housekeeping chores can be minimized if storage facilities are well planned. This does not necessarily mean a major remodeling job. Perhaps you merely need to reorganize the existing space to make it more efficient for your home and family. Or perhaps the addition of shelves, a cabinet, or a piece of pegboard mounted on the wall might add the convenience you are seeking. Start by evaluating your needs—the types of items you need to store, how much space they will take, whether you use them frequently or seldom—to determine the type of storage you need.

Many old cabinets, chests, and cupboards that you might find in resale shops could lend themselves to a process of modernization. Interiors can be painted, papered, or covered with fabric. Exteriors can be painted, antiqued, or refinished; moldings can be removed, repaired, or added; hardware can be replaced if it is unsightly or of poor design. Such pieces can be used in bedrooms for clothing and bedding; in bathrooms for linens; in living and family rooms for books, games, stereo components, or TV; in dining rooms for table linens and silver.

Perforated hardboard is one of the least expensive materials you can use. Mounted on the wall, or in the back of cupboards, it can unclutter almost any area. In the kitchen, pots and pans and gadgets can hang on pegboard hooks; near the work bench, they can hold small tools; in the garage, garden tools can be arranged in an orderly fashion on a pegboard.

To add storage space in a bedroom, buy several inexpensive wicker hampers and place them on shelves one above the other. In addition to its usefulness, this is also an interesting decorative feature.

A shoe bag hung on the wall in a guest closet makes a good receptacle for mittens and gloves. Put it at a height that children can reach, and identify the pockets so that each child will recognize his own.

If your kitchen cabinets are already packed to overflowing and you have not an inch of wall space to spare, consider the ceiling. Try suspending an old spoked wheel encircled with long hooks to hold those pots and pans and molds that are too bulky to hang neatly on pegboards or that have handles too long to tuck away in cupboards. A suitable wheel might be found in a junkshop, bought for a few dollars, and cleaned up in next to no time. Add some inexpensive hooks and a chain from the hardware store, hang up your pots and pans, and you have a decorative center of interest in your kitchen.

Doors to cabinets and closets are often overlooked as potential spots for food, tool, and utensil racks. Simple for the average handyman to make, these can be decoratively arranged and framed in full view of the room or concealed on the inside of the door. If you live in a new home or in an apartment, door racks can take the place of a pantry.

You can conceal your tape deck, tapes, and records behind a door, all neatly stored and easy to reach. Build a frame from 1 × 6-inch pine boards and screw it to the back of the door. Be sure to make the frame narrow enough to clear the doorknob. Use metal angle plates to strengthen frame.

The sewing center at left disappears when not in use. The tabletop folds up over the shallow cabinet, and the legs drop down to form part of the frame around a picture mounted on the underside of the table. It is so compact you would hardly guess it was more than a framed picture on the wall.

Tall, thin shelves on roll-out casters will fit a space between refrigerator and wall. This one is 4 inches deep and 24 inches wide. Four casters are concealed below the frame with ½-inch clearance. The shelves are ¾-inch plywood edged with 1¼-inch strips to hold cans in place. Cost: $12.

This storage unit is designed for the man of the house. Build the base cabinet first and fit it with slide-out trays for folded clothes. Plan the width for the space available; make it 36 inches high and 20 to 24 inches deep. Build the upper unit all the way to the ceiling and about 12 inches deep.

To create a toy chest like the one below, build a large plywood box, then build two grids from 1 × 2-inch wooden strips to fit inside and support the plastic-dishpan bins. Run two strips of 1 × 2s from front to back to support each bin. Add 1 × 2-inch facing around the front edges, and paint.

Thrift in practice

Recognizing a bargain when you see one is an important factor in dollar-wise decorating. This does not necessarily mean that you should look for the cheapest price, but that you should be reasonably certain you are receiving good value for every dollar spent. Also, if you patronize home furnishings stores, department stores, and building supply companies that have a reputation for reliability, you can be confident that they will back up their merchandise. If you find any reason for dissatisfaction, such firms are most likely to make a fair and honest adjustment.

If fabric is to play an important part in your overall decorating plan, shop carefully before making your purchase. Although it is sometimes possible to find sizable remnants at a fraction of the original cost of the fabric, never let yourself be coaxed into buying fabric just because the price is drastically reduced. If it is not the color, or texture, or pattern you need to carry out your decorating scheme, it is not a bargain.

Shop for the best quality you can afford when you're seeking that bargain. It is poor economy to invest in an item of furnishing that will receive hard and constant wear unless it is of good enough quality to stand up to that hard wear for a reasonably long time.

Some kinds of home furnishings are regularly placed on sale at certain times of the year. These include floor coverings, furniture, fabrics, bedding, and bed linens. Watch your local newspaper for sale advertisements, and shop to see what savings you can make and still get just what you want to carry out your decorating plans.

Before you are tempted to go on a shopping spree and buy new furniture that will fit into your decorating budget, make the rounds of the secondhand stores and thrift shops in your community. You may find pieces which, with a little work on your part, could be real money savers and, at the same time, add interest to a decorating scheme.

From time to time, there are sales of unclaimed freight, post-office sales, and warehouse sales. Watch your newspapers for advertisements of these events; some are also announced on radio and television. Attend auctions and house sales, too. You may find just what you want, and at a price that is well within the confines of your budget.

Many homemakers have discovered that there are treasures available for a song when old mansions and public buildings are demolished to make way for a modern building project. Solid oak, mahogany, or walnut woodwork can often be salvaged and restored to excellent effect as paneling, shelving, room dividers, or bookcases.

An old door might be cut down to a size you need with stylish effect. Marble bathroom fixtures are sometimes for sale at bargain prices, as are handsome old shutters, lighting fixtures, and hardware such as doorknobs, drawer pulls, and hinges.

Storage in a space-shy bathroom can be solved by installing metal standards and shelf brackets, and adding ½-inch plywood shelves. Add a few accessories and plants to make your storage area decorative as well as functional.

It's a snap to turn a one-drawer file cabinet into storage for records and a mobile stool or table as well. Mount plate-type casters on the bottom corners of the cabinet. Cut motifs from adhesive-backed burlap and apply to sides and top.

On the following two pages you will find five budget items ▶ that are simple to make, low in cost of materials, and yet appear tasteful and luxurious.

The tall sleek divider is made from ¼-inch clear plastic and ⅛-inch smoked plastic, and rests on three slotted strips of wood. The shelves provide a perfect background for accessories of bright color and contemporary styling.

The way-out wine rack is made from nine sheets of acrylic plastic. Eight of the sheets are cut half way through to make interlocking joints. The ninth piece is glued to the top for a serving area.

To make this contemporary chandelier string nylon fishline between six triangular sheets of acrylic plastic glued to a central cylinder. Add a lamp fixture, hang, and light.

The sliding-paneled private-eye window has a 30 × 36-inch wooden frame to house the textured plastic. These sheets are available in a variety of colors.

For the bases of a zigzag table, cut four 18 × 24-inch pieces of black plastic. Interlock two pieces to form an X, then glue in the clear plastic shelves. For the top, glue on a 24 × 36-inch piece of ¾-inch clear plastic. The surface should be coated to prevent damage.

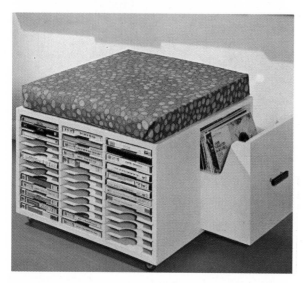

Mix the old and the new

As you set out to furnish—or refurnish—with budget ideas, do not be afraid to mix the old and the new. Remember that skilled professional designers do it all the time. Avoid a hodgepodge, of course, but plan deliberately to place a few "reclaimed treasures" into a contemporary scene. Your only limitations need be to mix casual with casual, formal with formal, for pleasing results. Acquire an eye for seeing old furniture with new potential, such as converting an antique chest to a coffee table or a banister railing to a divider. If you approach your budget hunting-shopping expeditions in a spirit of adventure, you can turn what might be a dull and boring task into a delightful experience.

Be a do-it-yourselfer

Your own handiwork, used to embellish your home, brings a special kind of personal satisfaction. You can project yourself into the decoration of a room by means of a remodeling project or a handyman job, something you have stitched up on your sewing machine, furniture you have refinished, or an attractive display of the family's handicrafts or hobbies. It takes only average ability plus ingenuity to join the ranks of satisfied do-it-yourselfers.

Top: A handy serving cart can be built for about $18. Nail a frame together using hardwood boards. Add narrow molding strips along the top edge of each shelf, making a rim to hold cargo aboard. Cover the top with ceramic tiles, attach decorative handles and ball-type casters. Stain, varnish, or paint.

Middle: A 2-foot-square unit with a drawer for records and indented shelves for tapes can be a useful mini-library for music. Use ¾-inch plywood for everything but the tape section; for that, use ½-inch plywood for the partitions and ⅛-inch hardboard for the shelves. Add casters for mobility.

Bottom: An old trunk is newly fashionable when it's relined with wallpaper or fabric and painted or antiqued to match or contrast with other room furnishings. If the top is flat, it can serve as a coffee table in addition to its obvious storage function. Search junkshops for one of these treasures.

If you succumb to the urge to poke about in secondhand and thrift shops, you may be repaid for your curiosity by finding some worthwhile objects waiting to be discovered. Let these pieces prompt your imagination to transform old discarded objects into furnishings and decorative accessories.

Do-it-yourself projects offer the budget decorator both savings in cash and the very special satisfaction that comes from using your own skills and your own ideas to produce a useful and attractive item for your home.

The pictures in these pages represent many different do-it-yourself projects; some are simple and require very little skill, others are more advanced and call for some basic carpentry. None of them involves the outlay of large amounts of money; all offer practical solutions to problems of space and budgeting.

Depending upon your decorating needs, your skills, and the amount of time you can devote to it, there are projects for everyone. You may want to add bookcases to a plain wall, make new draperies with valances to match, re-cover upholstered furniture for a fresh color scheme in the living or family room, rebuild a headboard to fit an oversize mattress and box spring. Budget project ideas are endless. Adapt or revise any of the suggestions illustrated here to fit your needs.

Top: The familiar rattan chest turns desk when it is opened and fitted with a piece of plywood in the lid to provide a smooth surface for writing. Sturdy chains on each side hold the lid firmly in place. The wall-hung chest-desk and the matching rattan stool cost about $68.

Middle: A serving unit that holds table linens and flatware was cut from an old chest. The top and sides were painted, then waxed. Wrought-iron brackets were mounted on the wall to support the unit, and a pair of mirrors, with the frames sprayed black, were hung above.

Bottom: You can gain both decorating impact and a full wall of storage space with a treatment like the one at right. The cabinets below afford storage space, and the open shelves show off collector's items. Colors in the paisley wall covering are picked up in the open shelves and in the cabinet base.

Discover The Advantages Of Buffets For Informal Entertaining

Add to the party scene in your home by including a buffet. It can be the conventional type or one you devise yourself to suit your space and your decor.

A large party, especially, calls for the buffet-style serving of food, since few homes today have dining rooms or tables large enough to seat more than eight or ten guests comfortably. When food is displayed on a buffet, guests may serve themselves and then take the plate to a convenient place to sit or stand. For a buffet meal it is a good idea to serve foods that can be eaten with fork or fingers—no knives. With too many utensils guests have to perform uncomfortable balancing feats.

A buffet is also useful for parties of smaller size. It frees the host of the tasks of carving and of serving the guests individually. And, in this day of diets, guests can help themselves to the foods they want, in the amounts they choose. When the guests have served themselves, everyone returns to the dining table to eat in company.

If buffets of the style you like are too expensive to fit your budget, make one yourself. It need be no more than a shelf mounted on a wall to serve the purpose. Or search the thrift shops for one that can be renovated with paint, varnish, and possibly a new top of tile, vinyl, or one of the self-adhesive papers. If you do use a paper covering, better give it a finishing coat of clear lacquer for extra durability.

Look over some of the buffets and built-ins shown on these pages; also, see *Dining Areas* for a style to suit your taste. If you decide to make a buffet, look over the wall space to see what size you can fit into it, and take some measurements. Then, with measurements in hand, visit a lumberyard.

If you plan to paint the finished piece, you need not buy the highest quality lumber. Only if you plan to do a cabinetmaker's job, with a fine wood finish, is it necessary to buy top-grade wood. Ask your dealer to advise you on the quality of wood to buy for the job you plan, and have him cut lumber to lengths you require. For help on building such a piece, see the sections later in this volume on *Built-Ins*.

Although buffets need not have drawers, they're a good place to store silver, linens, and other tableware, and it is very convenient to have such items close to the table where they'll be used. One way to provide drawers inexpensively is to buy unfinished chests of the right size, line up two or three, and add a top that will cover and join them together. If you plan a shelf-type buffet, ready-made drawers are available that can be suspended underneath.

Here's a buffet so simple in style that almost any handyman ▶ could assemble, stain, and varnish it to add to convenience in entertaining in a family room or other informal setting. Essentially a series of shelves, it would fit in well with other furnishings in Early American style.

When planning a buffet—and its menu—do take into consideration how the seating will be arranged. Perhaps you will have card tables or tray tables already set up nearby, so that guests can sit down. In this case, you may plan a buffet and table setting to include foods that will be eaten with knife and fork. Napkins, silverware, plates, and serving dishes should be placed in an order convenient for the guests.

Buffet flower arrangements are easy to improvise, and food is more inviting when accompanied by decorative fruits and flowers such as those that add appeal to this harvest feast.

You can add a wall-hung serving unit to your dining room in a single afternoon, even if you're an all-thumbs non-handyman. You do not need to do any carpentry or even pick up a paintbrush, so there is no time-consuming cleanup to do after you have completed the job.

First, visit a kitchen dealer and pick out three or four cabinets that will harmonize with the furnishings of your dining room. You will find a wide range of sizes, styles, and finishes to choose from. Those pictured in this buffet measure 6 feet long and 2 feet high overall, and have a walnut finish.

When you get the cabinets home, unpack them and screw them together, following the instructions included with each package.

Attach a 1 × 2-inch cleat to the wall studs so that the buffet will hang 7 inches from the floor; rest the unit on top of the cleat, push it against the wall, and screw it to the studs.

If your budget is tight, you can, of course, purchase unfinished cabinets and do the painting or varnishing job yourself.

For a tremendously practical scarproof and stainproof top—and one that looks luxurious as well—use a slab of ¼-inch slate. First, cut a piece of ¾-inch plywood to fit the top—or have your lumber dealer cut it for you. Screw it to the cabinets, and place the slate slab on top.

Slate may be purchased precut to whatever measurements you specify; or you might be lucky enough to find a school blackboard in a wrecking yard, if your community has recently been replacing old school buildings. If the blackboard you find is too large, you can have it cut to size by a marble dealer.

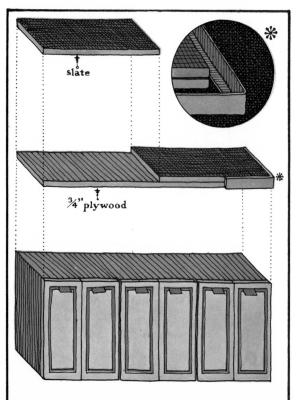

slate

¾" plywood

The last step in assembling the buffet is to install a strip of 1 × ¼-inch aluminum or stainless steel around the sides and front of the top, covering layers of slate and plywood. If the hardware of the cabinets you purchase does not harmonize with the metal strip you use, replace it to give a custom look to the finished piece.

Diagrams illustrate the steps to be taken in finishing the top of your buffet, as described above. To achieve a professional look, take care in bending the metal strip so that it turns the corners smoothly. It may then be secured in place by bonding it to the plywood strip with epoxy cement.

Your new buffet will be even more useful if you install extra shelves in some of the cabinets for storage of tableware requiring only shallow space. Linens, silverware, trays, and mats will be accessible without lifting out and re-sorting piles of things each time you set the table. Shelves that slide out on runners attached to the side walls of the cabinet are even more convenient. They may be purchased ready-made in a variety of widths and depths that will fit most standard cabinets; or you can make them yourself if you are a fairly experienced handyman.

Install cup-hanging hooks for efficient use of space. A lazy Susan on one of the shelves will enable you to store a number of small items (liqueur glasses, for example) and still get at those stored at the back of a cabinet without reaching in over other fragile items.

This beautiful buffet, with loads of storage space, takes up 8 feet of a wall space in a dining or family room and permits you to keep dishes, linens, and silver where you need them most—right next to the dining table.

If you do not have this much wall space, or do not need as much storage as this unit provides, you may, of course, alter the plan to suit your individual requirements.

Before you begin construction, check on the kinds and sizes of louvered doors that are available locally, since their dimensions—and multiples of them—will be the major factor determining the height and length of the finished unit. By using ready-made louvered doors, you can achieve a professional effect easily and inexpensively.

The relaxed way to entertain

You'll entertain more easily and be a relaxed hostess if you use buffet-style service. Guests, too, enjoy a party more if they do not feel they must burden you with requests for service.

The first essential for serve-yourself parties is an adequate buffet. Build your own to get the exact size you want.

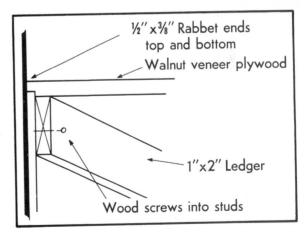

½" x ⅜" Rabbet ends top and bottom

Walnut veneer plywood

1"x2" Ledger

Wood screws into studs

Diagram shows how to install a wall-hung buffet like the one pictured on this page. First step is to build a simple box, using 3/4-inch walnut-faced plywood of measurements to accommodate the size and number of louvered doors.

Install shelves to suit your storage needs; fasten louvered doors in place with top and bottom hinges. Anchor unit to wall with ledger strips (see detail), and add finishing touches: walnut tape on edges, flat black paint, oil on walnut surfaces.

Make room for a buffet if you like to entertain and prefer relaxed, informal meals that do not overburden the hostess operating without help.

Even a shelf of approximately 16 to 18 inches in width and 4 to 5 feet in length can do the job. If you use the space beneath for storage, you will save yourself a great deal of time setting out dishes, linens, silver, and glassware for your party.

Choose a spot for your built-in buffet that is as close as possible both to the kitchen and to the dining table. When you are preparing for a party, you will be glad of any extra steps you can save on those numerous trips from kitchen to buffet, and your guests will appreciate finding a place to sit near the serving area. Of course, your choice for a spot for a built-in will be determined largely by your room arrangement.

Paint can camouflage the bulk of the buffet if the room is small. Paint the piece the same color as the walls and woodwork if you want to disguise its size and make it "disappear."

If the setting is more spacious, consider finishing the buffet in wood tones to match or harmonize with those of the other room furnishings. This is easy to do, now that you can purchase plywood faced to match walnut, mahogany, and other finishes.

Look what paint color can do to reduce the apparent size of a built-in piece such as this roomy buffet. The color, somewhere between beige, green, and yellow, is one that tends to "recede," makes you think an area is roomier than it really is. Painting the buffet to match walls and woodwork goes a step further in helping to reduce its apparent bulk in a tight area.

By making use of ready-made louvered doors like these, any competent handyman could build this floor-installed rather than wall-hung model.

The top might be surfaced with laminated vinyl of a matching hue, or with paint finished with a coat of clear protective varnish so food spills will not mar it. Other materials good for buffet tops are ceramic tile, marble, and slate.

Impressive and unusual hardware, such as these door pulls, can do much to give a built-in that luxury look. And today's choices in hardware of this type are nearly endless. Styles to harmonize with both modern and period furnishings come in both budget and luxury price ranges.

BUILT-IN LIGHTING
How To Enhance Furnishings And Background With Concealed Lighting

Built-in lighting combines beauty and function. Designers have discarded old-fashioned lighting ideas and have flooded the scene with exciting, imaginative built-ins that fit into homes of every size and every architectural style.

No longer are fixtures solely centered in the ceiling of the room. Now they are placed wherever they best fit the needs of the room and its occupants: length-of-the-ceiling fluorescent panels that dispel gloom; soffit strips that diffuse light and cast it at wide angles wherever you need it; decorative canopy and drop panels that provide both local and general light; suspended lights; recessed panel lighting, and a variety of other illumination techniques.

This is true, too, for wall fixtures. They come in a variety of shapes, sizes, and designs: valances that highlight draperies; brackets that set light splashing up and down a wall; cornices that hug the ceiling and send light flooding downward; luminous wall panels; under-rail lighting that enables you to brighten the area beneath a window and set off a view; and frame lighting and wall lighting to enhance the effect of decorative accents.

The list is seemingly endless. The net result is a choice of illumination techniques that enable you to combine beauty—decoration—with function—lighting.

What you can do with wall fixtures
Wall lighting is of three basic forms: valance, bracket, and cornice. Each is easy to install and has many uses in the home.

(1) *Valance.* This, the most popular wall unit, is always used over a window, and often sweeps the length of a room. The unit is installed above the draperies, with the fluorescent tube placed at the top of the valance faceboard; this allows a small amount of light to flow up and be reflected down from the ceiling, and a large amount of light to flow down. To avoid reducing the amount of light available, make sure the fluorescent tube shines in front of the drapery. For best use of a valance, make the faceboard 6 to 10 inches deep and paint the inside with a flat white paint. The outside of the faceboard can be as decorative and stylish as you wish.

(2) *Bracket.* A variation of the valance, bracket units are fitted onto a wall and cast light up and down. Because no drapery is involved, the tube should be placed close to the wall and should be centered on the faceboard, allowing equal amounts of light to flow up and down. Again, the inside of the faceboard should be painted flat white.

Soffit lighting is great over a kitchen sink and an adjacent ▶ kitchen-office counter. In this installation, light is thrown both down onto work areas and onto ceiling to supply general illumination for a kitchen-family room arrangement.

Plan on installing two rows of tubes if your soffit is standard counter width (18 inches), three rows if the counter is wider than average. If you require maximum brightness, use a louvered diffuser. Parabolic aluminum reflectors behind tubes will effectively increase their brightness by concentrating all of the light downward onto a work area.

Most utility companies offer free analysis of your home wiring needs. If you are remodeling, check with them. You may find you need one of the following to avoid an overload on present service: three big entrance wires; 100-amp circuit box; additional circuits; more outlets, lights, or switches.

If you have a kitchen whose arrangement is similar to this one, you may want to use a ready-to-install fixture like this one. It clips together easily. All you need do is attach clamps (A) to the wall, then clip the track (C) to the clamps. Fasten the corners with the remaining clamps, labeled (B) in the picture directly above.

Next step in installing the new overhead lighting panel is to nail 2 x 4 hangers to the ceiling joists. If the joists run parallel to the beam, fasten hangers as shown in the picture above. If the joists are perpendicular to the beam, use a long hanger on the inner edge of each side. Weight of suspended beam requires that hangers be securely installed in the ceiling.

Nail and glue to the beams the strips that will hold plastic diffuser material in place. Leave a 6-inch gap in the top strip if you plan to use the flexible type of plastic; you will need only the lower strip if you use the rigid type of plastic diffuser material. Once the strips are in place, you are ready to nail the sides to the hangers as shown.

Paint or finish the outside of the beams; then paint all of the inside surfaces with flat white paint to get maximum benefit of light reflected on bright surface. Lay roll of plastic in gap of upper track. Feed it to the far end of the beam. Unroll the rest and tuck it in. When it is necessary to remove for cleaning or installing new tubes, reverse the operation.

(3) *Cornice*. This unit differs from valance and bracket in that it directs all its light downward. The unit is placed at the junction of the wall and the ceiling. To achieve the best lighting results, make the faceboard 6 inches deep and set it at least 6 inches from the wall. Whatever the measurement, make it consistent, that is, the same depth as width. To obtain the best reflection, paint the inside of the faceboard white.

The above three are the basic wall built-in units, but there are others you can use for dramatic decorative effect. Highlight cabinets and shelves with sparkling fluorescent lighting. Install frosted glass shelves to obtain a pleasing luminous effect. Then place attractively arranged accessories—small statues, or a collection of trophies—on the shelves. Or place local lighting inside a built-in bookcase, preferably one with a glass top. This is a most effective method of lighting a painting or wall accessory.

As a backdrop for an abundant display of potted ferns and plants, use a luminous wall unit. Install large plastic panels set into wood or metal frames off from a wall, or as a divider. Or provide general light under the window to turn an ordinary window into an exciting panorama of nature at her most mysterious—at night, when the hidden wonders of the garden are spotlighted. With such staging you stamp yourself as a dramatic home decorator.

Ceiling units—a type for every need

As wall built-ins combine decorating beauty with lighting function, so, too, do the many ceiling units. Effectively used, they cast light on the normally dim areas of the rooms, adding to the usefulness of every inch of your kitchen or any other room in the home.

(1) *Cove*. As its name implies, cove lighting is often used in small recesses or alcoves. The cove is usually made of wood, metal, or plaster; it should be at least 12 inches below the

Exercise your imagination with the new materials available at lighting specialty shops, and you can design handsome lighting units to fit the specific needs of any room.

The 3-foot-wide beam above shows how one family licked the old "one center fixture" problem in their kitchen. Now, after the installation of a new lighting panel, the whole room is brighter and the work area is much better lighted.

If you wish, you can purchase wall-to-wall lighting that comes in a package, ready to install. Plastic diffusing material is the major ingredient. This plastic is both light in weight and flexible; others available are rigid. Both types can be used successfully with either fluorescent or incandescent lamps. Use the number of bulbs or tubes required to give the kind of light you need—at least two 30-watt fluorescents above a sink, as in this installation.

An additional tube installed under the cupboard at right of sink would improve working conditions on the counter beneath.

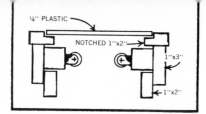

There is no need to restrict yourself to just one built-in lighting idea at a time. As shown in the picture and line drawing, three treatments—wall brackets, shelves, and panel of light—can work harmoniously as one. To construct, build the wall bracket as shown in the drawing; then put the panel in the stereo cabinet. (You can use the same instructions given for the ledge project below.) Build your shelves deep enough to accommodate a fluorescent tube, and recess plastic inserts even with tops. To get upward and downward light, simply leave the shelves open at the bottom.

ceiling, with the center of the light 4½ inches from the wall. This prevents excessive glare. Because of the soft quality of the illumination, cove lighting should be used in small rooms or alcoves with high ceilings.

(2) *Luminous*. These installations offer a soft, diffused light that is uniformly distributed around the room and can be controlled by a dimming device. The luminous ceiling, is, in fact, a false ceiling of plastic panels hiding a row of fluorescent tubes. For the most effective installation, paint the ceiling cavity with several coats of flat white paint; this will ensure the best possible light reflection. The depth of the cavity is optional, after complying with the National Building Code stipulation that an allowance of 7 feet 6 inches must be·made between ceiling and floor of a room. Space above that height can be used for installation of luminous units. Generally, a cavity of 12 inches in depth is best for the home. Many luminous units can be purchased packaged ready to assemble. The units include channels, flexible plastic, and all the hardware needed.

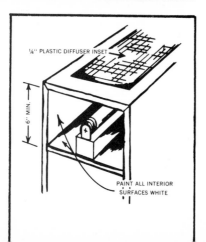

What was simply a narrow ledge behind the sofa is transformed into an exciting display area when light comes from a recessed panel. Light shining upward gives solid objects an etched quality, and the cut-glass collage in the foreground sparkles with reflected light. As shown here, make your light box at least 6 inches deep and center a fluorescent tube toward the top. Recess a translucent plastic panel so that it is level with the top of the enclosure; let it just rest in place, to facilitate cleaning and tube-changing. Using the same idea, you could design a similar unit with bookshelves or cabinets.

As the picture illustrates, a strategically placed cornice can visually raise a low ceiling or highlight your draperies, murals, or pictures. It can help give a room a warm, comfortable glow while at the same time heightening the decor of the whole room. When you build such a cornice, make your shielding board so that it is at least 6 inches wide and 6 inches out from the wall. Then center your tube or bulb 3 1/2 to 4 inches out from the wall. Here, louvered plastic diffusers hide the light source from the conversation area while bolstering the general illumination of the room.

(3) *Floating canopy.* Similar in principle to a luminous ceiling unit, a floating canopy is installed below ceiling height and over the section of the room you wish to highlight. Here a dimming device is essential. If the canopy is above a wall panel of photographs or pictures or over the television set or stereo, too much light will destroy the desired effect. Correct diffusion throws the emphasis on the area you want to show off.

(4) *Coffer.* This illumination technique involves a cove bent into a circle, installed in the ceiling. The coffer unit is especially effective used at the main entrance of the home, where it casts a welcoming glow. This effect can be enhanced by fitting the coffer with colored fluorescent lamps. To tie the entryway to the general decorating theme of the home, pair lamps or tubes of different colors—colors that are part of the scheme of both the entryway and the first room a guest will enter.

(5) *Canopy and drop panel.* Similar to the floating canopy, the canopy and drop panel provides light where you need it—both local and general. It is encased in wood or metal.

No missteps here. This is a smart safety idea as well as a very attractive decorative one. A single light—either fluorescent or incandescent—outlines all three steps on these open-riser stairs. You can mount a light in any spot where it will work without being seen. This is just one of many ways you can use built-in lighting. By adding such lighting, you can decide where it should go, how it should look, and what it should cost. Use it to bolster general illumination, to accent a decor—or both. Dramatize a textured wall, enliven a drapery, heighten a ceiling, or as in this case, light your stairs.

Bathrooms in older homes seldom have adequate lighting near the mirror where it is needed for dressing the hair, applying cosmetics, shaving. Of the various kinds of lighting available for this use, overhead, concealed, and built-in types are probably best, since they cast light down, not into eyes.

Here, overhead ceiling fixtures do a good job of both general illumination and specific light above wall mirrors.

Soffit lighting is used imaginatively here to perform the double task of illuminating a bathroom attractively while providing maximum light for those using the wall mirrors.

The soffit should be as long and as wide as the counter and about 8 inches deep. Build deeper for more light cast down, less outward. Install two rows of tubes if soffit is standard 18 inches wide; three rows if it is wider than that.

Dimming devices—new lighting magic

A dimming switch or rheostat can provide a room with many moods at the touch of a finger. This variable light switch, usually mounted on a convenient wall, can be connected to any type of lamp, from fluorescent to incandescent. A lamp suspended over a dining table can be brightened during the main course, dimmed for dessert and lowered still more for a romantic mood. A variable

To install the hall lighting pictured, follow the diagram immediately below. Install a double row of tubes in space between ceiling joists. You can attach them to sides of joists or to bottom of the subfloor. Distance between tubes should be about 1 1/2 or 2 times the distance from the tubes to the sheet of diffusing material.

Use T-shaped hardware or strips of lath to suspend translucent panels; this way, you can raise them easily to clean them or to change the fluorescent tubes.

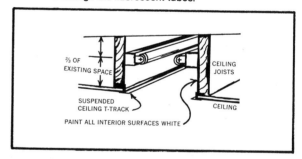

Long halls used for storage are very efficient but can be a decorating problem unless they are adequately lighted.

One of the best solutions to the problem is shown here—a series of recessed ceiling panels that shed broad, even bands of light. This kind of installation does away with protruding wall fixtures that consume space in narrow halls.

light in a television viewing area is almost a necessity. When the set is on, the surrounding light should be low but present. When the room is used for purposes requiring more light, the installation can be turned up.

Outdoor lighting, too, can benefit from a variable switch. Turned low, lights can create an intimate atmosphere for evening garden parties. At its brightest, outdoor lighting is an effective deterrent to prowlers.

A rheostat switch can be installed as easily as the conventional on-off type, yet adds innumerable lighting variations. The use of colored bulbs can enhance still more the desired effect. By experimenting with colored bulbs, natural bulbs, and with switch variations, a room can be transformed almost completely from one mood to its opposite. Most do-it-yourself handbooks have instructions for the installation of this switch.

Sketch shows installation technique for valance light in bedroom pictured at bottom of the page. Note that tube is placed at least 2 inches out from draperies so light will be evenly distributed as it falls downward onto fabric.

Sketch illustrates how a wall bracket can be used to direct light both upward and downward, bathing a brick wall, appropriately chosen for a room with a beamed ceiling. Allow at least 3 inches between wall and tube, 2 inches between tube and shielding board. Mount board at least 10 inches down from ceiling, but no more than 65 inches up from the floor.

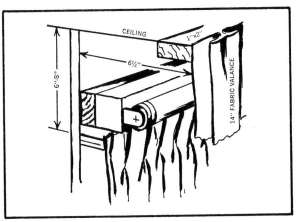

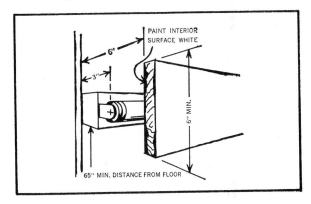

Cleverly installed valance lighting puts 24-hour sunshine on soft bedroom draperies. To get even upward distribution of light and avoid an unpleasant hot streak on the ceiling, it is necessary to install shielding material (see sketch) of at least 6 inches in width. It should run all the way up to the ceiling, or else be closed off at the top.

Indirect lighting here not only increases general lighting at the fireplace end of a modern living room, but also enhances the appeal of an exposed brick wall by casting light on it to emphasize its texture and pattern as important features of the decorating scheme. Ceiling-hung light fixtures focus attention on the large plant for maximum decorative effect.

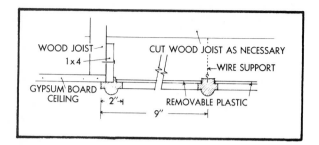

WOOD JOIST
1 x 4
CUT WOOD JOIST AS NECESSARY
WIRE SUPPORT
GYPSUM BOARD CEILING
2"
REMOVABLE PLASTIC
9"

Sketch at left illustrates how simulated ceiling skylight at lower left was installed. A portion of gypsum board ceiling was removed, an inset box frame built to brace ceiling joists and form a brace for the light fixture.

This unusual lighting installation gives soft dining light and adds design interest to the room. A simulated skylight, controlled by rheostat, has four fluorescent tubes recessed in the 4 × 4-foot unit that provides any amount of light—dim or bright. Light is softly diffused through removable translucent plastic panels. Each tier of this black wrought iron chandelier holds six candles. For poorly lit rooms, a simulated skylight adds a hint of outdoors.

Where to install built-ins

The uses to which you can put built-in lighting are limited only by your imagination. Every room in the home, every large expanse or small alcove, can accommodate a built-in unit. Before you select a unit and look about for a place to install it, ask yourself several questions: Where do you need light? What type of light do you need—local, to focus attention on an object, a grouping, or a small area; or general, over a wide area? Will that unit be the only one in the room or area, or will you have several units? Having answered these questions, you can determine what built-in unit will meet your needs.

Window or wall lighting enhances the decor of a room, focuses attention on the texture of draperies, the pattern of wallpaper, or the drama of an artistic picture wall.

Ceiling light, more general in nature, casts a blaze across the whole room. This is especially true of luminous light used in large areas. But you can also use drop panels in order to highlight a small area or a single object. Soffit light is another good example of the double nature of ceiling light; it is very effective for illuminating shadow areas on kitchen counters.

Accessibility for maintenance purposes is an important fact to keep in mind. Bulbs burn out, and this should be taken into account when the light enclosure is constructed. Fluorescent bulbs, especially, can be a problem.

Lighting in a kitchen is probably more important than in any other room of the home. In this one pictured below, the entire ceiling is lighted. The ceiling material is fiber glass, and the panels are supported by wood beams. Fluorescent tube lighting was installed between the original ceiling and the fiber glass panels. Before renovation this kitchen had a very high ceiling and inadequate lighting. A lighted suspended ceiling solved both problems.

Fluorescent tube lighting beneath the wall storage cabinets sheds light on the work counter below. This type of lighting is especially suitable for rooms that have a generous amount of subdued wood finishes and for rooms that get little natural light. It adds convenience to a work area that is occupied so much of the time.

Wood ceiling beams extend down one wall, creating a recessed area between counter and wall. The recessed area is used as a planter for green foliage plants that add a lively note to the severe contemporary styling of the built-ins.

For gardeners in the family a whole new world has been opened with the availability of artificial lights for plants. Supplementing or substituting for sunlight, these plant sun-lamps can form the basis for a built-in planter-and-plant-light combination that will allow the cultivation of exotic and exciting plants in some special corner of your home. Call your local greenhouse for information on the kind of plants you can use and the specific type of light you will need.

BUILT-INS

Gain The Extra Space You Need With Built-In Units

Built-ins are adaptable space-savers that can easily be designed to suit your decor and just as easily be custom tailored to your storage needs. The simplest type of built-ins are single-purpose, easy-to-make units, such as cupboards or bookcases, that even a beginning carpenter can construct. More ambitious builders should consider the many possibilities offered by combinations of built-in units. A dull kitchen wall, for example, can become an interesting and useful showplace if it is filled with cupboards, shelves, and a china closet. In a small area a clever planner can substitute a wall lined with convenient built-in units for a cramped room filled with furniture. Using wood paneling to extend walls into your rooms, you can create space to be filled by built-in drawers, closets, shelves, or even a cozy bunk, perfect for a child's room or a guest alcove.

For anyone living in close quarters built-ins are the ideal way to utilize precious space that would otherwise be wasted. A box spring and mattress can be set into a frame with built-in drawers and shelves to make use of space beneath a bed; corner built-in bookcases and revolving half-round kitchen shelves can fill awkward areas usually left empty; windows can be framed with built-in bookcases and window seat combinations that provide extra storage, extra seating, and the illusion of extra space. Even unused doors can serve a purpose by becoming shallow built-in display areas.

All built-in storage units are essentially a group of basic boxes or boxlike components held together by a frame. They can be attached to a wall or constructed so as to stand on the floor. If you do the carpentry yourself, a good built-in can be a money-saving answer to your storage problems. Even if you hire someone to do part of the work, a built-in is probably the most attractive budget-saving way to store your possessions. You don't need lots of tools, time, or money to build a handsome, useful unit for your home. For reassurance, read the practical step-by-step directions on how to build the units that are shown on pages to follow.

Don't hesitate to embark on installing a large built-in unit only because you think it means a long, inconvenient period of clutter, sawdust, and shavings all over the place. Even large units can usually be built and partially finished in the workshop, then fastened to the wall in one easy work session.

First decide which room in your home has the floor space to spare and is most in need of additional storage. The kind of unit you decide to build will be influenced by the room in which it will be installed.

Then consider the size and shape of the items to be stored. Will space be needed for hanging garments, for unwieldy things like golf clubs or carpet sweepers? Will a series of adjustable shelves be adequate?

Combining open bookshelves above with a series of cupboards below, the built-in unit in this living room is a simple but adaptable type of storage. With little change, except for installing doors above as well as below, the same type of unit could go into the kitchen, family room, master bedroom, sewing center, home office, or children's room. This handsome unit was constructed of warm-toned natural oak, here set off by a color scheme of restrained reds and greens. Comfortable furniture and adequate lighting complete this room, adding to a relaxed reading atmosphere.

The fine art of camouflage

Camouflage is one of the many functions that can be performed deftly by built-ins, and windows are the architectural feature most frequently in need of disguise. In older homes particularly, windows are often awkwardly placed or poorly proportioned. Newer homes, too, frequently have window problems. A functional modern casement window, for example, may not be suitable to your plans for a traditional or period-style decorating scheme.

Camouflaging a window with a built-in not only blots out an unattractive architectural feature but also provides additional storage space. Such a double-bonus idea is well worth considering by anyone interested in home improvement.

Much of the carpentry involved in such a project can be done by the average handyman. The more you can do at home, the greater your savings. Even if you hire a carpenter and do only the finishing yourself—painting and staining—a built-in may be one of the biggest decorating bargains you'll find to change the face of an important room and to increase its beauty and convenience.

Step 1 is to build the basic frames that will flank the window. Make them with 1 × 10-inch pine boards. Build them flat on the floor, then stand them up in the corners. Frames should be about 3 inches shorter than the height of the ceiling for ease of handling. Plywood arches will later cover the entire top portion and hide any difference in height between bookshelf units and ceiling. Fasten the frames to the wall with screws sunk into the wall studs. Extend the lower front section of the frames with 7-inch boards to form the cabinet and its top or counter. This will extend the length of the entire wall or built-in unit, and should be of fairly good quality wood to save lengthy sanding and filling.

Step 2 involves building in the rest of the cabinets that will run under the windows and hanging plywood arches. First add 1 × 3-inch facing to the front edges of the cabinets. Next cut plywood arches (a power saw is best for this job), which go up in two pieces, joined in the middle with a wood cleat. Nail and glue the sections in place, checking with plumb to see that they are correctly aligned. Give your work a professional look by filling over nails to cover hammer dents.

Step 3 begins with building the cabinet doors from 1 × 2-inch pine and decorative hardboard. The flush doors used for this unit are the easiest type to make, since they are really just rectangles with no special edge treatment. But they take some care in hanging, because they must fit exactly to look well. Start by measuring door openings. Cut two doors for each opening, about 1/16-inch larger both ways than the actual measurements. Hold door panel in place with hinge side tight against facing. If door opening is not exactly square, plane to fit.

Step 4 completes the basic installation with the hanging of shutters over windows. Install the shutters unfinished first, using scrap pine facing as a spacer to align them. When you are sure they hang correctly, remove the shutters and take off the hinges before painting. In this way you will avoid getting spray paint in the hinges—and also avoid marring a finished surface in the test installation.

Before you go on to the final stage of painting (or varnishing), be sure to sand down carefully any rough spots in the wood, fill in knot holes or nail holes, fill cracks (if any) in basic frame. You should always put on a primer coat when painting new wood before you apply the essential two (three are even better) coats of enamel. Be sure to allow each coat to dry thoroughly, and then sand lightly before applying the next coat to assure a good bond between coats. When painting is complete, replace hinges and install door pulls in a style to suit room.

Only some simple tools are necessary

Few basic tools are required for constructing a built-in similar to the ones pictured and described here. You will need a good hammer, a handsaw, screwdrivers of two or three sizes, a chisel, a plane, and a plumbline (to help you make certain that upright pieces are exactly vertical and to be sure that the shelves are truly horizontal).

A power saw is helpful. If you don't own one, you can rent one for a weekend, use it to complete all the sections on which it is useful, and assemble them at a later time. Other tools also can be rented when they are needed only briefly.

In a room that had no unbroken wall space, the effect of at least one solid wall (plus an enormous amount of valuable storage space) was gained by installing a good-looking, functional built-in wall cabinet.

Using louvered shutters to cover existing windows was a much better choice than using glass curtains, because shutters allow light to filter through but do not visually break up the space. The broken-up effect was the original flaw in the room's architecture that the project sought to remedy.

Installation of cane panels in doors and the use of curved lines for plywood fronts were decoratively appropriate for a room furnished with traditional pieces. The arches were painted the same color as the cane in order to better relate the top and bottom halves of the unit. If it were desirable to make the room appear larger than it is, it would be preferable to paint a built-in unit of this type to match the walls so that its bulk would be less conspicuous. Painting the end walls in a color different from that of the other two walls tends to bring them visually together.

The open shelves above are ideal for books and for displaying decorative accessories, art objects, floral arrangements, and greenery. The enclosed shelves below provide storage space for all those items important to family living that you like to keep out of sight but readily accessible.

BUNKS

How To Use A Time-Tested Method To Save Bedroom Space

When a bedroom is too small, take a lesson from those old masters of space-saving—the designers of the ship's cabin and the railroad's Pullman car: stack the beds one on top of the other.

The too-small bedroom looms large as a shortcoming of the average modern home. For children and teen-agers, play space and room to stretch out on the floor are important attributes of a bedroom. The number one problem solver for a skimpily proportioned bedroom is the bunk. Available in a wide variety of standard furniture designs, bunks are an economical way to enlarge a room's useful space.

Even more efficient as a problem solver is the custom-built bunk, a unit built to fit the space available. And it need not be expensive if there is a handyman around who has minimum carpentry skills and can wield a paintbrush once the unit is built.

In addition to the obvious space-saving effected by stacking one bed atop another, the custom-built bunk can have the additional virtue of furnishing extra storage space. Closets in modern homes are seldom large enough to accommodate all the possessions of two youngsters sharing a bedroom. But under-bunk space can work minor miracles by supplying a convenient place to stow precious gear that just can't be squeezed into the community closet.

But don't limit yourself to under-bunk space. If you have one side of a room free for the double bed, try to add a double closet. Divide the closet in two and give each child an area for hanging clothes, with a shelf compartment above. This arrangement frees under-bunk space for more adventurous clambering. And if you include a ladder, you double the adventure possibilities.

Even if each child has a bedroom of his own, the bunk can still be a desirable piece of furniture by offering sleeping space for the occasional overnight guest without occupying valued floor space at other times. Youngsters like to climb to bed, and an easily installed guard rail can eliminate all worries about accidental tumbles.

Depending upon the wall space available, the built-in bunk can offer—in addition to space for sleeping—room for a bookcase, a stereo, a television set, or, as pictured at the bottom of the facing page, an extra closet where apparel on hangers can be stored.

If the built-in bunk has a base of sturdy plywood and a good-quality foam mattress, springs will be unnecessary—and you will save both space and money.

Use easy-care materials for bed linens

When you select a fabric for spreads and bolsters, make sure it is machine washable and requires little or no ironing. If there is no worry about wrinkles or stains, the bed makes a good spot for playing games—especially if you install wall-mounted lights as has been done in the boys' room shown at the upper right of the next page.

The visual appearance of spaciousness will be greatest if a bunk is painted to match or nearly match the wall color. Accents on vertical lines will help make a low ceiling look higher.

Here is a good example of the bunk's capacity for saving space. You get "clear the deck" results and free the floor for young boys' activities when you stack one bed above another. By installing a floor-to-ceiling support wall and covering it with pegboard, you achieve an attractive bulletin board where children can hang both decorative and useful objects, plus catchall storage space with an attractive but inexpensive wicker hamper.

Both bunks were designed for box springs plus mattresses, but you could use foam mattresses alone for young children and install door or drawer storage beneath the bunks.

You can build these bunks in three separate sections in your workshop, assemble them in the bedroom. This kind of construction makes it possible to remove the bunks and take them along if you contemplate a future move to a larger home. This is a practical solution for two youngsters sharing a room.

Space-expanding tricks were employed in furnishing the room. The vertical lines of wall paneling at the far end of the room are echoed by black paint on the exposed end of the wall section; and the color scheme is simple—essentially red, white, and black, with neutral beige tones for bunk covers, wicker accessories, flooring, and wall paneling. Both of these devices further the goal of making the room appear larger than it really is.

Ideal for the long, narrow bedroom is this unusual bunk. Attractively tailored in appearance (important to growing boys, who reject all feminine frills), it is also admirably practical; it supplies generous storage space for clothing and toys in its ample sliding-door closet and roomy drawers at floor level. Foam mattresses on bunks are easy to fit, good for young backs.

You build this model in component parts, then fasten them together in the room where they'll be placed. If you can build a plywood box, you can build this project, which is, in essence, just a group of boxes. Save yourself work—and the necessity of purchasing or renting expensive woodworking tools—by preparing an accurate plan that includes exact measurements of all major lengths of lumber. Then have the lumberyard cut boards to your specifications, ready to put together.

Supported by the closets that divide the two floor-level bunks is still another bunk, reached by the simply constructed ladder. Equipped with lamps, it is a great anytime hideaway for reading, studying, listening to records. And it's perfect for extra accommodations when there are overnight guests.

Decorating is of the homespun variety, masculine enough to please and be practical for growing boys. Everything was selected to be both durable and easy to keep clean. Plaid bunk covers (they don't show soil easily) are nicely related to the big black and white vinyl tile squares with which floor is covered. The tile is another easy-to-keep-clean feature that cuts down on worries over spills. The red throw rug that adds a warm touch of color can be machine washed and dried.

When you plan furnishing of rooms for boys older than, say, four or five (younger, if they show real interest in color), let them take part in your choices. Youngsters have a special feeling for bright colors and patterns, and they're entitled to a voice in the decorating decisions for their own rooms. It's possible today to combine child-pleasing color schemes with down-to-earth practicality and easy care. Perky fabrics can also be washable; many drip-dry and are ready for use.

On these two pages, you will find more examples of the built-in bunk, designed to fit existing space exactly. Both would lend themselves to modification to make them suit your youngster's space and accommodations requirements.

Curtail playtime destruction and disarray

Sturdy furniture that can take abuse is a must for furnishing the rooms of growing boys. And sturdy bunks, inexpensive to build, rank high on the list of nearly indestructible children's furniture. If you have set up house rules that put the living room off-limits for rough play, it's important to provide some place where the youngsters can feel unrestricted. What better spot than their own bedroom? It will be easier on your house and on your nerves.

This simply constructed double bunk, especially suited for a boy's bedroom, is largely built of 2 x 4's. They are layered so that the lower unit projects farther into the room than the upper, leaving convenient storage space against the wall. The slatted walls used here could be replaced by solid ones and equipped with shelves, if you prefer.

This unit has been painted rather than given a wood finish because painting allows the use of less expensive grades of lumber. It is also easier to refurbish the unit with a fresh coat of paint when dents or mars make it unsightly—or when the occupant's color preferences change.

Installing a guard rail would make the upper bunk completely safe even for a very young child, and the matching ladder provides easy access. Wall lighting fixtures in a lantern design are conveniently placed for reading in bed, and can be switched on and off without getting out of bed. (To obtain plans for building this bunk, refer to PP 2120 HP 3607-1 in your reference listing.)

Variations of bunkbed styling put this built-in model in a slightly higher price category than is customary. Nevertheless, the unit offers a great deal more than the average amount of storage space. Drawers below will hold bedding and clothing, and the cupboard will accommodate larger and bulkier items.

Since this built-in unit contains only one bed, the wall space above it and on either side can be used effectively for shelves to store books and display decorative objects.

An always popular nautical theme is set by hanging an authentic life preserver on the wall and mounting a ship-model clock next to it. The red and white color scheme will appeal to boys of all ages, and the plaid fabric used to cover the bed and bolsters will withstand hard wear. The painted finish can be renewed by applying an additional coat when the inevitable scuffs and chips appear.

These bunks provide storage facilities for each child. There are four large drawers under each bed that can hold bedding, clothing, toys, and games. The shelf attached to the divider panel is a good place to show off a collection of dolls, toy soldiers, or stuffed animals.

The graceful curves of the cornices above the built-in beds soften the severity of the room. The same curves are repeated in the border design that trims the window shade. In addition to general lighting, there is a wall lamp above each bunk. The wall-to-wall shag carpeting adds textural interest. By using bunks rather than the usual beds, there is maximum space for a play area. When a child's room is organized as well as this one, it encourages children to maintain it in a neat and orderly fashion.

A bunk that saves floor space has been finished in a dark wood stain that matches the wood-paneled wall behind it. Beneath the bunk are convenient, capacious drawers, suitable for storing toys, clothing, or linens. A steel shelf under the window has been sprayed yellow and serves as a desk and bookshelf. Orange and yellow accents add warmth to the predominating cool greens. Vertical blinds at the window are adjustable. A contemporary globe floor lamp lights the desk area.

CABANAS

Add Convenience And Beauty To Your Pool Area With A Cabana

Americans borrowed the word *cabaña* from the Spanish, to whom it meant a hut, simplified it into just plain cabana, and used it to mean a lightweight beach shelter resembling a small cabin, with an open side facing the sea. In recent years cabanas have grown in popularity as more and more families have invested in swimming pools of their own. Today they are even more familiar as poolside structures than they were at the beach, and their functions have been expanded to suit the American love of informal entertaining.

Cabanas can and should be both functional and handsome. If they are in harmony with other construction features of the landscape plan, and if they also provide a comfortable area where you can dress and undress, shower, fix and serve light refreshments, and store swimwear and beach towels, you have all the basic requirements for a useful and

attractive structure. A cabana can be all these things for you, plus a pleasant retreat for just relaxing.

If there are no shade trees near the pool, the shade requirements can be fulfilled by the cabana itself or by building a lean-to extension on it.

Also important for comfort is the inclusion of a floor surface that is not heat-absorbing—outdoor carpeting, a wood deck, or a stretch of green grass close to the swimming pool—for the comfort of barefooted users.

The cabana can follow any architectural theme you choose. In planning, you should also consider whether you wish to equip it with showers, with a small kitchenette, and with storage for cooking and serving utensils connected with poolside entertaining. Unless your pool is close to a service entrance of your home, the cost may be worthwhile.

◄ Natural wood fencing and a redwood platform for sunbathing and cookouts have set the style for the cabana shown at left. Round forms are always less costly to construct than those of a square or rectangular shape. The cabana reminds us amusingly of a barrel, but its tropical-island appeal is reinforced by the grassy roof—which is appropriate to the nature of the overall setting.

Since some protective and camouflaging structure is necessary to house the machinery that operates the pool, the structure can be expanded to provide for a dressing room.

This tent-style poolside structure reminds one of those once set up by Arab chieftains near the battlefield. It is eminently suitable in any tropical or subtropical climate.

Metal posts support the pitched roof and the series of curtains that may be opened or closed, according to the wishes of those who want to escape the sun's full rays.

Dressing room and shower facilities are supplied by an adjacent permanent structure. But a place for changing into or out of swim togs could (in a less luxurious setting) have been provided by a curtained-off area at the rear of the tent.

CABINETS

What You Need To Know To Select Good Cabinets Or To Build Your Own

There are innumerable uses for cabinets in the home: for storage in the family room, living room, bedroom, and kitchen; as dual-purpose furniture, possibly as a seat and a storage chest, or as an occasional table or coffee table. And there are many types of cabinets: kitchen cabinets; those mounted on legs or on the wall; and combination cabinets with both doors and drawers. Whatever the use, you should know what you are getting. And if you are making your own, you should be aware of what shortcuts in quality will cost you in the long run.

Basically, a cabinet is any off-the-floor box, supported on legs or mounted on the wall. Cabinets can be made of wood, bark, metal, ceramic, or plastic; they can close with a lid or door panels fastened with hinges, hasps, or catches. Some cabinets are painted, refinished, or antiqued; others are covered with leather or fabric.

How to judge cabinetwork
Judging quality in the products you buy is often a complicated and difficult matter because you can not always see costly workmanship and materials. But with cabinets and other types of cases, you can make expert decisions if you are aware of the construction techniques.

Drawers in quality pieces are constructed with well-cut, well-fitted dovetail joints, and the sides are smoothly sanded and waxed.

Look for glue blocks in the corners under the drawer, placed there to keep the bottoms securely in place as the wood expands and contracts with temperature changes. Check to be sure that the joints have not been merely rabbeted and stapled together. This is a good test of quality construction. If the joints are stapled together, you can be sure the cabinet will not take even the ordinary pushing and pulling that occurs with use in most homes.

Be sure also that dovetail joints are cut cleanly and fitted tightly. If they are not, it is a sure sign that the drawer will not be sturdy. Note also whether the sides and inside are smooth or rough and splintery. This is another good test of the quality of the construction.

Remove a couple of the drawers and look at the construction inside, noting, as you do so, whether there is a friction-free center drawer guide. There should also be a wooden stopblock to prevent the drawer from hitting the back of the cabinet, and to keep it lined up properly with the other drawers.

Cabinets of poor quality have center drawer guides of wood, and lack panels between the drawers that would prevent wood dust from the guides from dropping into the drawer beneath.

Opening the cabinet doors in this kitchen is like reaching for a ▶ bouquet of garden-fresh flowers. These hand-painted sprays give a custom look to tall and narrow space, provide a bright and cheerful contrast to the deep tones of the wood finish. When a kitchen is fully equipped and well planned but looks drab, a fresh decorating scheme is your best answer.

Ingenious use of the moldings, trims, hardware, paint, and stains now on the market can give an uninteresting kitchen a new look. The most ordinary of cabinets can blossom with a little pampering. Try a scrubbable wall covering to give a lift to cabinet doors. Ceramic tiles glued on doors in an improvised pattern lend a custom character to mass-produced cabinets.

For the reluctant artist there are punch-out flower sprays in wallpaper units—delphinium or daisies might be dashing.

Learn to evaluate the quality of furniture. The interior finish is the key to the kind of workmanship and the amount of time spent on a given piece. Although the inside will never be as finely finished as the outside, you will find that it is painted, stained, or waxed in high-quality pieces.

Be sure to examine the hardware. Handles and pulls should be easy to grasp and firmly attached. On high-quality wood furniture, the hardware will be harmonious with the style and, in reproductions of period pieces, of a design contemporaneous with the era of the original.

Learn to identify woods. Mahogany and walnut resist shrinkage, warping, swelling. For unusual strength look to mahogany, oak, and walnut. The woods that take finishes best include beech, birch, mahogany, oak, gum, walnut, and maple. Softwoods include cedar, fir, pine, and spruce.

You will notice at once the sharp contrast between construction details of the chest above and the one pictured at left.

The poorer quality piece above is rough looking, has exposed boards that are crudely finished, neither stained nor waxed. Nails have been pounded deep into wood, with no filler to smooth the surface. No attempt has been made to conceal hammer indentations. Notice, too, that the joints are merely two boards butted together and nailed in an uncraftsmanlike manner.

Friction-type door catch is cheap, but it wears out much more quickly than the magnetic type, which is well worth its slightly higher cost.

In your own carpentry projects, learn to conceal nailheads. Countersink nails with nail set. Next, fill depressions with stick shellac melted on a spatula; press it into place.

The backs of chests, buffets, desks, commodes, and unit cabinets should be screwed to the frames. In furniture of quality, the backs are sanded and stained.

The length of screws for fastening the back to the walls depends upon the thickness of the bottom board and the strength necessary for the joint. The screw with an unthreaded shank must be just long enough to reach through the bottom board. Basic screws used in this way are flathead, oval-head, and round-head screws.

To be sure that screws hold in the end grain of a piece of wood, drill a hole near that end and plug it with a wood dowel. Coat the dowel with glue before tapping it in. The dowel will then anchor screws driven through it.

Another mark of well-made furniture is the supported back with bottom edges fastened for extra strength.

The back of the chest pictured below has been neither sanded nor stained. It is warped, split, and cracked. It is not fastened at the bottom. Openings of this type make furniture vulnerable to dust, moths, mold, and fungus infestation.

Well-finished backs are glued as well as nailed in place. Glue makes a bond in two ways: either by entering the openings of porous material and giving mechanical adhesion, or by adhering tightly to nonporous surfaces through contact tension. Wood to be glued must be dry and free of oil, grease, or wax. Any old glue should be sanded off, and dust removed.

Adequate clamping is necessary during drying, to hold the glued parts firmly in position and to prevent warping.

A back piece such as this one, which overlaps the sides of the unit, is a clear indication of poor workmanship.

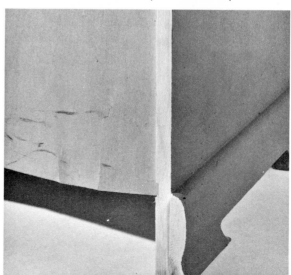

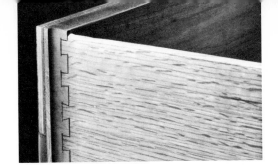

Drawers in high-quality pieces, such as the one at left, are constructed with precisely cut, tightly fitted dovetail joints. Drawer sides should be smoothly sanded and waxed. If a wood or varnish filler is used, the drawer must be completely dry before it is placed in position.

When you examine a piece of furniture for quality of craftsmanship, look for glue blocks in the corners on the bottoms of drawers. These small but important bits of wood prevent the drawer bottoms from falling out as the wood dries and shrinks, and from warping when it expands during damp weather.

A drawer may be said to fit well if it moves from side to side without more than ¼ inch of play when pulled out halfway.

The drawer at left is an example of inferior construction methods. The joints are rabbeted (also referred to as the common mortise). In this case, the joints are stapled—proof positive of unprofessional workmanship. This type of joint will pull apart after only brief use.

The sides of the drawer have been neither sanded nor waxed, but merely run through a "joiner." Notice the gap between side and back, which will permit entry of dust, moths, fungus, and mold. To avoid binding, all drawers should be an inch narrower than the space between the bearing strips.

The drawer pictured at left has dovetail joints—usually the best type of fitting. But here the dovetails have been carelessly cut, and the joints will be easily dislodged by moving, a hard jerk, or a sharp blow.

Both inside and outside of the drawer are rough and splintery, indicating careless construction.

If a piece of furniture has good lines and high style and suits your taste, but shows evidence of shoddy construction, you might consider repair and rebuilding—if you take the cost of these projects into account in the price paid. Unless you can do the work yourself, you had probably better reject the piece.

In this chest the sign of inferior construction is the absence of dustproof panels between drawers. In the operation of a drawer, wooden guides rub against guide strips and produce a certain amount of wood dust. Lack of separating panels lets this dust drop into the drawers below.

A simple way to dustproof drawers that have begun to come apart is to round out the corners with plastic wood and then sand them.

Drawers that are not of the so-called lip type do not need to fit as tightly as do flush drawers. The disadvantage of this less expensive type of construction is that the drawers are not dustproof and mothproof.

One way to determine whether or not a dresser or chest of drawers is of top quality is to remove several of the drawers and examine the inside. Well-built pieces will have friction-free center drawer glides.

Three types of drawer glides that give good service are the side slide; the center slide, which must be accurately fitted and allows less clear height inside the drawer; and the metal slide, which is easy to install and is not subject to swelling or shrinking.

Drawers of the so-called flush style should be fitted with wood stop blocks at the back of the chest to ensure that the drawer will align properly when it is closed. Such blocks can be installed easily.

Look also at the interior of the cabinet. Although the inside need not be as finely finished as the outside, it should at least be sanded, stained, or waxed, and the joints or nails should be concealed. Be sure to examine the hardware. Handles and pulls should be easy to grasp and firmly attached. On good pieces they are harmonious with styling.

Lastly, check the back of the cabinet. The back should be screwed to the frame and be supported and fastened along the bottom for extra strength. In good-quality furniture, the back is sanded and stained. A sure sign of poor quality is a back that overlaps the sides and is only nailed in place.

You may not be in a position to afford furniture of the highest quality, but if you keep all the above tests in mind you will know exactly what you are getting and how long you may expect it to last.

Make your own
The cost of quality cabinets today is often prohibitive for homeowners on a limited budget. But with a few tools, some wood and nails or screws, and some paint or fabric, you can easily make your own—especially if you have a workshop. First, start with a plan. Determine the type of cabinet you want and note the space you have available. Then put your measurements down on paper.

How to make drawers
All but the most experienced handyman or cabinetmaker should do all the preparatory work for one section of each drawer at the

A butted joint (shown top left) is one of the easiest to make; however, it is also the weakest of the wood-joining methods. To make a butt joint, cut the stock square, then fasten the two sections together with screws, nails, or glue. It is a good idea to attach angle plates on the inside walls of cabinets for added strength.

The rabbeted method of joining wood (shown top right) makes a much stronger joint than the butt joint—especially if stress will be from the top down. The width of the cut is half the thickness of the stock, and the depth matches the stock to be joined. Glue the parts together and clamp them in place while they dry.

Mitered corners (shown below left) are more difficult to construct, but stronger and neater than butt joints. Measure accurately, then cut the wood stock at a 45-degree angle. Fasten the two sections together with nails, screws, or glue. If you use glue, clamp the sections together while they dry.

Dowel joints (shown bottom right) require accurate measurement. First step is to clamp the two wood members together so that the edges that will take dowels are exposed. Mark a pencil line across both surfaces for each dowel, using a try square for accurate marking of dowel placement. With a depth gauge, mark the spot on each line where dowel holes are to be made. Use a prick punch or an awl to mark the drilling points. When the holes have been drilled and the dowels inserted with glue, the two members should line up. Spread glue along the exposed edges of both members and clamp.

same time. Cut the wood and repeat the same grooves. Do this for the two sides of the drawer, the back, the front, and the bottom. Cut all the pieces to the exact size, remembering to allow 3/32 of an inch between the sides of the drawers and the inside frame—thus the front and back pieces will be 3/16 of an inch shorter than the frame plus the amount you allow for the dovetail.

Then cut the guides: one for each inside panel of the frame, and a center guide. Position the guide so that it will fit into a rabbeted groove on the outer side of the drawer. The underside of the drawer need not be rabbeted, but you can screw a runner to the underside that will fit into the guide.

Before gluing, assemble the five pieces of each drawer as a final check. When you are satisfied with the fit, disassemble the pieces and lay the front side down with the dovetail joint uppermost. Apply glue, then put the side panel into the slot and drive several thin nails into the joint. Repeat this procedure for all joints until the drawer is assembled.

Next attach the drawer glides or guides to the inside frame with three 1-inch flathead screws, and countersink. Then check whether the drawer fits. If it binds, remove the drawer and sand down the guide.

To control the depth to which the drawer enters the cabinet, attach a bumper strip behind the guide at the back of the frame, and also stop the rabbet on the side of the drawer just short of the front edge. In this way you can ensure that the drawer fits flush in the cabinet.

Spline joint (shown top left) is strong and sturdy. It is generally used in table or cabinet construction. Basically, this joint is made with a plywood strip, which is glued and "wedged" into the dado cuts as the edges of stock are glued and bar-clamped during the drying process. It takes a little longer to make than other joints.

Rabbeted joint (shown top right) is not only strong but is an excellent way to conceal a cabinet back. To make, cut ¼-inch rabbets the thickness of the back in the sides, top, and bottom framing pieces before assembling. When finished, simply glue the parts together—or, if you prefer, use nails or screws for a somewhat stronger bond.

Slip blocks (shown below left) strengthen as well as add more glue surface to any joint. They are especially useful in strengthening butt joints. Cut out blocks, then apply glue and push them into place with short, sliding motions until they sit tightly against both pieces of the stock.

Combination rabbet and dado joint (shown below right) is a good one to use when joining sides of a cabinet to the bottoms. You can further strengthen the joint by driving in finishing nails at an angle after having glued the two pieces together. Use clamps to achieve a tight bond. After the joint has dried, fill nail holes slightly more than level with wood putty or plastic. Let filler harden, and smooth surface with fine sandpaper. If you want a natural finish, use stick-lacquer or stick-shellac to fill in nail holes. Melt stick with a lighted match or an alcohol lamp and drop melted plastic into the nail holes.

What kind of doors?

Your choice of door will depend on whether you want the hinged or sliding type. Each has its own particular advantages and disadvantages.

Hinged doors can be made flush with the cabinet or lipped, to protrude outside the measurement of the frame. But flush doors exaggerate any construction errors. They may show an open space along the door edge, or jam against the cabinet frame.

Sliding doors are quiet, efficient, and attractive. But they open only half of the cabinet at a time, and unless the door is well constructed, they jam easily.

Whatever type you choose, assemble the door as you would a drawer, cutting the sides and then the panels, and assembling the complete door to test the fit. Then, as with the drawer, disassemble the pieces, lay one side on edge, and glue it. Repeat for each side until the door is complete, and perhaps clamp the joinings until the glue has set.

When making a hinged door, select hinges strong enough to support the weight of the door and to prevent sticking. Some hinges can be concealed; others lie on the face of the door and add a decorative touch.

Choose latches with the same care. They should not be weak and liable to bend or loosen with use. Note also that when you use a decorative hinge, the latch should match it in style.

The method you use in making a sliding door unit depends upon the amount of time and money you are willing to invest.

If you want the cabinet to close completely, you can use wooden strips to make a two-space channel, or rabbet the lower frame, or you can buy a molded channel to do the same job. If, on the other hand, you do not want a completely closed cabinet, but will slide a single panel so as to leave half of it open at all times, you can purchase a molded track for the single door to slide on.

The use of wood stops is the easiest method and the least expensive. Assuming that the doors are ¼ inch thick, you space the three ¼-inch wood strips 5/16 inch apart and glue and nail them to the frame. The additional 1/16 inch is sufficient to allow the door to slide easily.

Rabbeting the lower frame is almost as easy, but it is more costly because of the time required and the possibility of error. Repeat the above measurements, but drop a rabbet 3/16 inch into the lower frame. Any greater depth will make it hard to remove the panels.

Ready-made tracks and channels are simple to install and make the doors slide easily. Double channels of molded fiber or plastic are excellent for glass doors.

A tall cabinet combined with antique and reproduction furniture helps to create an overall atmosphere of elegance in a room of three basic colors—brown-to-gold, white, and green. The deep brown tones of the cabinet blend well with the tones of the chairs, the table, and the gold of the mirror and provide a pleasing contrast to the basic green of the walls and the drapes. Besides being highly decorative, the cabinet is also functional. Its upper half is used to display a collection of fine china pieces, and the bottom drawers provide storage for flatware and table linen.

This handsome armoire has a light antique finish and elegant hardware that complements its graceful curves and intricate wood carving. It was carefully designed to duplicate the style of cabinet used by Marie Antoinette and Louis XVI at Le Petit Palais, where the vogue for provincial decor in furnishings originated. The large armchair with velvet cushions and fur pillow is of the same period design. Today the style is known as French provincial or country French. The floor covering closely resembles Versailles parquetry, but is actually vinyl flooring that is installed square by square.

A "catchall" room is made newly stylish by virtue of the bold lions' heads of papier-mâché that decorate cabinets in an entry next to the garage door. Cabinets are of plywood with pine molding; glued-on manila rope outlines the designs.

After the rope was in place, a coat of gesso tinted with raw sienna was added. Plastic spray was applied over this. Designs were tinted with burnt orange, and another plastic coat was added. A final glaze of raw umber was the finishing touch. The eyes are of crystals with pupils painted on reverse sides.

The Far Eastern influence has been captured in the design of the sophisticated drawer pulls shown at left. Made of polished brass, the pulls have 3-inch centers; coordinating knobs that measure 2 inches across are available.

Hardware, a necessary convenience, need not be only functional. Well chosen from the fashionable varieties available today, it can take its place as an imaginative decoration.

How to make shelves

The shelving you select for your cabinet will depend upon the purpose the cabinet is to serve. Display cabinets often have glass shelves that help to show off the contents and to reflect the local light you install in the cabinet. Most cabinets, however, have either wooden or plastic shelves. Many can be bought to the width you need with the front edges already finished.

The methods of installing shelves vary to suit different purposes. For a kitchen cabinet you may want adjustable shelves, so that you can alter the height to fit the products you buy or the household articles you store. The adjustable feature is also useful for display cabinets, or bookshelves. But whether you want adjustable or fixed shelves, there are many types of installation available.

One of the simplest fixed types of installation is a metal bracket screwed into the back of the cabinet at shelf height, almost to the width of the shelf. A less simple type is an angle iron screwed into the back of the cabinet and screwed through the frame of the cabinet and into the shelf. In a variation of this type, a dowel or pin is placed beneath the shelf to replace the screw. Each method provides adequate support. If you do not want the angle iron at the back of the cabinet, you can fit a molding strip at shelf height and screw it into the inside frame of the cabinet. When doing this, it is best to install a thin molded strip the height of the cabinet to cover the cleat ends. Or you can support each shelf on a center wood support placed an inch or two back from the edge of the shelf.

In an apartment kitchen (or any kitchen lacking daylight), ▶ yellow paint simulates sunshine, and it is on tap the moment you switch on the lights on dark winter mornings.

Color-keyed and vinyl-coated wallpaper runs up the walls and across the ceiling to help establish the springlike yellow and green scheme, which is furthered by painted wood cabinets and wood panels above the sink that conceal curtain rods.

CAMOUFLAGE

How To Conceal What You Can Not Correct

Nature's use of camouflage can be seen in the changing plumage of birds from season to season, allowing them to blend into the landscape and gain protection against their enemies by becoming more difficult to distinguish from the natural features of their habitat.

The art of camouflage may be as valuable in decorating a home as it is to wild birds. Are windows badly placed? Does an ugly but indispensable radiator mar the appearance of a room? Is a ceiling too high or too low for pleasing proportions? Is the length of a room too great for its width?

To these and a host of other problems that may plague you as you plan a decorating scheme, camouflage is the solution. It may be impossible or just not feasible to alter the basic structure. But there is, if you will search for it, a way to camouflage the defect, to wipe it out visually.

Draperies, built-in cupboards, fool-the-eye wallpaper, and just plain paint are but a few of the ingredients with which tricks of camouflage can be carried out. The rooms pictured across the page show two examples of camouflage—used to disguise radiators. They are just a hint of the many capabilities of this strategy called camouflage.

Wallpaper is famous for the visual tricks it can play to improve the appearance of a room. Cut canopy fashion and properly applied, it can lower a too-high ceiling. Scenic and mural wall coverings, used to cover a badly placed door, can make it seem to disappear. The use of darker paper on end walls and lighter on side walls makes a long, narrow room more pleasing in its proportions.

Window treatments, too, rate high on the list of camouflage strategies. Floor-to-ceiling draperies plus a cornice can add height to a room; they can make windows look larger than their actual measurements, can space them or group them more gracefully than their architectural placement seems to permit.

Color, one of the most important tools of camouflage, can unify space magically. In a room with too many openings—doors, windows, archways—use of the same hue on walls, woodwork, and window treatments can almost blot out the chopped-up look.

The optical effects of color—warm colors advancing, cool ones receding—are strong allies in the color campaign. For example, a room without much natural light can seem lighter with walls and ceilings of pale pink or yellow; a too-bright room will cool off with light green or blue walls. Ceilings can be lifted or lowered and irregularities made less obtrusive through the uses of color camouflage.

More permanent than the other methods of disguise listed, but often the best of all solutions to architectural flaws, is built-in cabinetry. Use it to disguise faulty architectural details of many kinds, and gain new storage space as a bonus. Disguise or hide unpleasant structural features by building over them. Install a sham wall, closets, or a buffet to hide the unbearable faults of a room. (See also *Built-ins,* p. 666.)

Train your eyes to see how camouflage is used in other rooms pictured throughout the volumes of this encyclopedia; adapt ideas you find to suit the decorating problem in the room you seek to make more beautiful.

Many older homes have at least one window under or beside which stands a necessary but ugly radiator that presents a problem when planning a window treatment.

By combining a stylish radiator cover and draperies tailored to clear the top, you can often distract attention from the offending radiator—and perhaps even make an asset of it, if you are clever with camouflage.

In an inviting bed-sitting room, radiator covers were painted to match the walls and topped with seat cushions in harmony with the overall color scheme. Draw draperies meet the cushion; separate panels extend to the floor at the sides.

A tall radiator at the right of a living-room window was an ugly and dominant feature until this built-in structure was installed to hide it behind shutters and then go on to form a window seat and storage cabinet. The shutter-pattern wallpaper above the radiator unit suggests windows that, in fact, do not exist.

Inexpensive shutters of this type can be bought in a wide variety of sizes, or can be ordered to fit your space requirements. Easily installed and painted, they are a highly effective means of camouflage.

If you have a problem similar to this and are considering boxing in a radiator as part of your solution, be sure to provide at least a 3-inch space above the radiator to permit circulation of heat.

When space is not available in the kitchen or utility room for the storage of cleaning equipment and large appliances, it is time to improvise. Sometimes it is possible to borrow space from another less conventional area to serve the purpose. In the illustration, at right, a corner of a dining room (it could be a family room in your case) has been used to solve the problem, without even a noticeable change in the appearance of the room.

Simple panel doors were fitted onto borrowed space. The molding that separates the dado from the upper wall was run across the lower section of the closet doors; thus, when they are shut, there is no hint of the functional use to which the space has been put. Paint, too, fosters the illusion that this corner is just an ordinary wall of the room. Slim chains keep the doors from swinging too wide and damaging the walls.

Inside the bonus storage space, a pegboard wall helps the homemaker make maximum use of the closet. Easily fitted with L-hooks, the pegboard stores mop, broom, vacuum attachments, and other cleaning equipment, as well as fold-away serving tables.

An overhead shelf accommodates odd-shaped, bulky—as well as seldom used—serving pieces.

The Japanese, for whom living space has been at a premium for generations, have many useful lessons to pass on to Westerners when it comes to making a small house look larger, or when light is needed but a view is poor.

Here, bamboo screening blots out an undesirable view but allows daylight to filter in. A young, container-grown tree gives a garden effect to this end of the room and, with a pagoda lantern, lends an illusion of space.

For good light control, semi-opaque screens in lightweight framing (the Japanese call these shoji screens) pull across an entire wall to cut out strong sunlight.

Shoji screens are perfect for any interior that emphasizes Oriental furniture and fabrics. They are also versatile enough to blend with predominantly modern furnishings, whether of European or American design.

The view below shows what is behind the interesting shoji screen treatment pictured at left. This living-room feature, once so popular with homeowners and home builders, can present a real challenge to the homeowner who buys an older home and counts on decorating on a budget to update the house.

An alternative treatment might have been to use the seat as a plant shelf, installing a metal box to solve problems of moisture seepage when plants are watered, and hanging sheer curtains to screen out an undesirable view.

If the room has other light sources, shutters in upper and lower sections are another possibility. The open top half lets in light; the closed bottom half obscures the view.

Take Advantage Of Portable Furnishings In Temporary Quarters

Until the era of modern warfare, generals and officers often carried portable furniture with them on military campaigns, frequently using the same pieces throughout their careers. Used in pitched tents to bring some semblance of "home" to battlefield camps, campaign furniture has traditionally been designed for convenience and comfort.

The few authentic pieces of campaign furniture that survive in this country and are still available to private collectors are largely those dating from the Spanish-American and Civil wars. The most common items are trunks, lap desks, and collapsible and portable chairs of various types. The lap desk with a hinged top was a favorite of generals. For light, they used a candlestick with a screw-in holder that was easy to pack; for seating, folding chairs.

Campaign furniture had to be compact and preferably was collapsible, functional in the truest sense of the word to merit the effort of carrying it along to war. Today, these characteristics are equally important to enthusiasts for the functional in home furnishings.

Modern adaptations

With such a historical background, it is not surprising that professional decorators and designers of household furnishings, who often look to styles of the past for inspiration, have adapted and modified campaign furniture to fit today's style of living.

Furniture manufacturers offer lines of campaign furniture that include chests, tables, desks, and even complete bedroom collections. The items can be used singly as accent pieces or in groupings. Lines are simple and unadorned, except for brass hardware trim with a contemporary feeling. Hinges, locks, and handles are reminiscent of those on original pieces, but scaled down in size so that they are compatible with the overall design. The canvas "officer's chair" is perhaps the most popular piece of campaign furniture.

Campaign furniture collections are available in a variety of wood finishes. One of the most popular is derived from the Japanese campaign chest—a lacquered finish available in Chinese red, black, yellow, blue, and white.

A campaign chest with a lacquered finish in Chinese red highlights a black and white color scheme. The metal corner strips and recessed drawer pulls are adaptations of those used on sturdy portable chests that officers carried with them on their military campaigns. At that time, the metal corners and edges were used purely as reinforcements so that the chest would withstand rugged traveling conditions. Now, the metal trim is used primarily as decoration on these otherwise unadorned chests. Campaign chests, either the old or new versions, usually rest flush on the floor. The utter simplicity of the design, Oriental in feeling, makes these chests a welcome addition to contemporary, country, or traditional rooms. They are both functional and decorative and are available in a lacquered finish in a variety of colors, or in the popular natural wood finishes.

CANDLES

Discover Dozens Of Ways To Use Candles As Decorative Accents

Candles have a long and fascinating history. Representations of candles appear on ancient Egyptian tombs, and candlesticks have been found at Crete that date from about 3000 B.C. The first known fragment of candle dates from the first century B.C. Candles have always been important in religion, particularly in Roman Catholic and Jewish ceremonies. In addition to such ritual usage and the obvious use for lighting, candles at one time were made to serve as timepieces, marked off in twelve measured sections to time the hours of the day.

The utilitarian candle has long since been replaced by electric lights. But to set a mood of hospitality, nothing is more effective than the flicker of candles, their soft gleam flattering the faces of those who gather to share a friendly repast or an evening of conversation.

As accessories rather than functional elements of a decorating scheme, candles should be chosen for color, size, and style and given a proper mounting in candelabra suited to the table setting or to the decorating scheme of the room in which they are used.

Made of paraffin wax or beeswax (the latter kind being superior because they burn longer and do not drip or smoke), candles today can be purchased in a fascinating and amazing variety of sizes, shapes, colors, and scents. Whatever your decorating or color scheme, you will find candles to match or to offer a harmonious contrast.

Make your own; it is easy—and fun, too

Making your own candles can be fun—and economical, too. All you need is a mold and a wick. *Molding,* as the name implies, involves the use of a form into which the melted wax is poured, and a wick running down the center. Antique candle molds of the kind used during colonial days may still be purchased, and accurate copies of such molds are also readily available.

A simple way to go about home candlemaking is to save food cans and cartons of shapes and sizes that please you. To begin, remove both ends of the containers. Cut out a piece of heavy cardboard to serve as a candle base, making it a little larger in diameter than the container. Poke a hole through its center and pull a wick through, knotting the wick underneath so it will stay in place. Set the container on the base.

Now select a stick wide enough to lay across the top of the container; pull the wick up and tie it to the stick to keep it taut and centered. Pour a small amount of melted paraffin (colored and scented as you choose)

An unusually decorated dining room exhibits a Moorish ▶ theme executed with flair. Draperies of dramatic stripes hang from floor to ceiling, and an extension of the same fabric covers the ceiling and creates a stagelike setting for a highly polished table and leather-covered chairs.

Spanish also is the design of the chandelier, its votive candles in squat glass containers shedding a warm glow on an interesting table setting.

Important accessories on the table include three large candles in improvised containers, which are actually pewter-washed copper goblets with stems of varying lengths. Appropriate to the setting are shiny tin service plates, salad bowls of dark wood, and smoky glasses. In good contrast are the jewel tones of place mats and napkins, and an appetizing arrangement of fruits that serves as a centerpiece.

Illumination provided by the chandelier candles and the three in the centerpiece gives adequate light for a dinner for four, lends an Arabian nights charm to the scene.

Candles become a major feature of a good-looking table setting when they are large and set in brilliant glass containers that advance the total color scheme.

Resembling the frosted blue water glasses in size and shape, the candles are appropriate accompaniments to the casual flower arrangement in its straw container.

Green Fuji mums and graceful vines plus candles in blue containers are keyed to the color combination established by the handsome table mats and napkins of informal style. All elements of the table setting are chosen with regard for the modern room setting.

over the cardboard base and allow it to harden slightly. Then pour in melted paraffin to fill the mold to the desired height.

Another method is to pour melted wax onto wicks suspended from a metal support until there is enough wax coating to give the desired thickness; then roll the soft candle on a marble slab to make it uniformly round in shape.

The colored crayons children use are a good source of dye for coloring wax to whatever shade is needed to carry out your particular color scheme.

In both methods, the quality of wick is important. For best results, the wick should be purchased from a hobby shop, but you can also use a good grade of cotton twine soaked in boracic acid solution and then dried before use.

For candles of whipped texture, beat the warm paraffin with an eggbeater and ladle it into the mold immediately.

To remove candles from molds easily, immerse the mold in hot water for a few seconds.

Be careful when melting paraffin, since it is highly inflammable. Use a double boiler to melt it, and do not pour it in the vicinity of an open flame.

Candlesticks, too, may be made or improvised to suit special table settings and room decorating schemes. Inexpensive colored glasses are effective; so are glass caster cups. Save the cores from rolls of tape, apply a coat of liquid gesso; let dry, then paint any color you choose.

Candle columns in descending heights and various thicknesses are grouped on a flat tray, framed with graceful fern fronds, and given a focal point with a compact bouquet of button chrysanthemums. The linear quality of the candles makes them an interesting centerpiece even when unlit.

This arrangement was planned for a one-sided effect, well suited to a seating arrangement such as the one in the table setting pictured here. It could, however, be adjusted to a center-of-the-table arrangement by centering the flowers and ferns and grouping the candles around them.

When the dining room of this older home was remodeled to achieve a more contemporary effect, the unusual chandelier became an important part of the decorating scheme.

Of simple construction that would not be difficult to imitate, it is composed of chain links at ceiling level that support two vertical metal bars. These, in turn, support a cross bar drilled to accept modern candle holders made of wood blocks and frosted glasses fitted with votive candles.

The chandelier is appropriate in style to the mood of unadorned simplicity established by the handsome wood-paneled ceiling. It is hung low enough over the table to make it easy to light candles with long fireplace matches.

Also noteworthy in the decorating of this room is its essentially black and white scheme (dark furniture tones are close enough to black to be so considered), with color concentrated in a brilliant wall hanging whose predominant hues are red-orange with purple as accent.

Elements of the table setting repeat the colors in the wall hanging: place mats and napkins of red and orange; low centerpiece of tiny red, orange, and purple strawflowers, which lend themselves well to mass arrangement.

The black and white of the room itself are echoed by the low bowl in which the flowers are arranged and in the china pattern of white with a soft gray border.

This candelabrum combines the effect of modern sculpture with the charm of candlelight. The little votive candles in their glass containers of glowing colors are inexpensive. A candle of this kind will burn for about six hours—more than long enough to decorate a festive evening with guests.

To duplicate this, construct the candelabrum frame from lengths of 1/2-inch-square aluminum bar stock. Cut random pieces with a hacksaw and lay them out in a pleasing pattern; then fasten the joints with self-tapping metal screws inserted from the back. Use epoxy resin cement to glue on the plastic coasters that will hold the candles.

After the unit has been assembled, spray it with flat black paint and attach to the wall with metal angle brackets. Select candle holders to harmonize with your color scheme.

In art nouveau style, metal funnels, perforated and painted in vivid flower colors, are mounted on metal rods that resemble stems. They'll hold fat candles to light a porch or patio party in good garden mood. If the candles are to be used outdoors, the metal rods might be pushed into the ground or into a big tub of soil that will serve as a base, with the candle flowers set at varying heights.

If flying insects are a pest, use citronella candles to serve the double purpose of lighting the party and keeping bugs at a distance.

If wind is a problem, large funnels will keep short candles from blowing out. Perforations allow light to shine through attractively when candles have burned down below the tops of the funnels.

In a long, narrow dining room, sparsely furnished, the baroque design of a ceiling chandelier and the rope-twisted candlesticks on the table are in pleasing contrast to the architectural severity of the setting. A careful search of antique shops should turn up these once popular baroque items. Ornate chandeliers can often be adapted to your taste by simply removing or adding sections or pendants.

Antique fixtures of this kind, of Italian, French, Spanish, or Mexican origin, have been skillfully copied in modern electrically wired chandeliers. Flame-shaped light bulbs are available that give a somewhat flickering light nearly indistinguishable from candlelight. Because they are low in wattage, it takes a number of them to light a large room unless they are supplemented by candles on the table.

If bareness as a style of decorating appeals to you, and you like the exposed grain of wood flooring and furniture, consider the use of elaborately designed candlesticks or ceiling fixtures that resemble authentic chandeliers as appropriate accents to your overall scheme.

Also attractive in a setting such as this would be an array of candlesticks—placed on either table or buffet—of different designs and heights, but related, perhaps, in the material of which they are made—copper, brass, silver, wood. For the collector, it is a happy way to display and use treasures assembled over the years. Although we customarily think of candles in connection with dining-room decoration, they can be equally effective in any room of the home.

The dining room is by nature sociable, and the table should be set to invite relaxed, friendly, and gracious dining. This one, in appealing traditional styling, relies on designs of cherished china, silver, and crystal to evoke an elegant mood for a dinner party.

On a white damask cloth, tall, slender candlesticks of silver in a classic shape hold white tapers that are correct accompaniments to both candlesticks and table setting.

Although very few families today ever serve a truly formal dinner party in the old-fashioned sense of the term (with the full array of silverware, crystal, and china that necessarily accompanies that tradition), an air of formality can still be carried out pleasingly if not authentically.

Most guests will, in fact, be far more comfortable in the modified style of semiformal dining that is preferred today, with tables set—like this one—with elegance but without ostentation. To preserve the best of the traditional but to eliminate its more burdensome demands is today's goal.

When you use a symmetrical centerpiece such as this one of yellow roses, the flower arrangement should be equally attractive from all angles, and the centerpiece should be low enough so that each diner can see all others with ease. The candles should be tall enough so that the flame is higher than the eyes of the seated guests.

In choosing candles for a table setting of this kind, think color. Key them to the color of flowers, tablecloth, or china.

CANOPIES
Add Drama, Elegance, Or Novelty To Your Bedroom With A Canopy

Canopies undoubtedly originated as protection against rain, harsh sunlight, and flying insects. Throughout history they have continued to serve these functional purposes, but as centuries have passed they have also assumed symbolic and decorative importance. As a variant of the dome shape that has traditionally symbolized divinity, they were used by many ancient cultures as ceremonial shelters for kings and rulers, and in the Middle Ages they began to be used in various religions. In later years, the graceful arching lines of draperies inspired architectural and sculptural imitations that can still be seen in European palaces and churches.

Today's dramatic and decorative canopies bear little resemblance to their functional ancestors, but they are very like their symbolic and decorative ones, serving to emphasize, to set apart, and to focus attention on a special place. They are often nothing more than a way to introduce brilliant color and increase apparent ceiling height. Other variations on the canopy theme, depending upon the colors and fabrics used, can be highly romantic or the ultimate in elegance for a master bedroom.

If the use of a canopy as a major feature in bedroom decoration appeals to you, first give consideration to the architectural style of the room and the basic design of the other furnishings. For a canopy to achieve the maximum decorative effect, it must be in harmony with the total setting.

In a modern home with exposed brick wall as an important feature—as in the bedroom pictured opposite—a frilly canopy would look quite out of place. Instead, a sleek and tailored version has been chosen, its color coordinated with other furnishings to make it harmonize with the setting.

Another point to take into account, if you plan to install a simplified version of the canopy, is wall space. For best effect, the canopy should be installed on a wall not otherwise broken by door and window openings. If windows are present, the canopy ought to be centered between them. Asymmetrical placement is seldom the most advantageous one for canopies.

If the canopy takes the form of draperies above a four-poster bed, placement is less important; however, centering it on a wall is still desirable if permitted by the architectural arrangement of the room.

Although the canopy is traditionally a bedroom feature, in modern decorating its use in other rooms can be very effective. It can be employed as a fabric hood above a kitchen window, or as a canopied ceiling in an elegantly furnished dining room (an excellent way to lower visually a very high ceiling in an older home).

The canopied ceiling can be functional in still another way, as you will see in the basement recreation room pictured a few pages further on, where it hides ceiling beams, pipes, and so on and gives the room an amusing circuslike atmosphere. Coupled with canvas wall draperies, it creates a new room within existing space without requiring expensive construction.

As a solution to a wide range of decorating problems, the canopy in one version or an-

The ever-popular bed canopy has gone excitingly modern in this teen-ager's bedroom. The striking effect is created simply by installing tangy orange vinyl wallpaper on the wall and ceiling behind and above the bed. Trimly bordered in black, the paper is cut to exactly the same width as the bed.

A great idea for decorating a small room, the wall trim takes up no space, yet creates the effect of a dramatic headboard and canopy. Use one of the adhesive-backed papers and install it yourself to keep the cost minimal.

Although the colors used in decorating this room are lively, they have a no-nonsense practicality about them. It is a well-organized, pleasant, and easy-to-maintain retreat.

Brilliant hues used for the floor covering, bedspread, and wall canopy contrast with white walls and draperies.

By the choice of well-styled furniture that can grow with a child—perhaps even move with her to her own first home—the often heavy initial cost of furnishing a youngster's room can be amortized over the long years it will be useful.

other is well worth your attention. For help in choosing a style that will be most harmonious in the setting provided by your home, study the variety of canopies shown on these pages and adapt them to your particular needs.

A private world of one's own—that is, or should be, the goal when decorating the bedroom. Favorite colors and styles should be chosen for the decor, and canopies can be used very effectively to enhance the total effect of this room.

In rooms that will be shared by all the members of the family and their guests, the setting should be agreeable to a wide range of ages and tastes. But in the bedroom, no matter whether it is that of the master and mistress or of the very young, only the preferences and predilections of its occupants need be taken into account.

If ruffled elegance is your choice, the bedroom is the perfect place to indulge yourself in feminine furnishings. If all else is sleekly modern but you like Victorian antiques, by all means have them.

Fit for a princess, this regal room makes precisely matched stripes a focal point of its decoration. The tailored canopy creates the effect of a classic tester, yet because of its diminutive size, it is inexpensive to make and easy to install.

Elegant poles that fit into wall sockets support the canopy and end in finials of sophisticated design. Striped fabric covers a lightweight plywood frame extending out about 2 feet from the wall, directly above the head of the bed.

A more frilly canopy treatment for a young girl's bedroom makes lavish use of ruffled curtains. These could easily be made with ready-made panels and valances.

If you use a plywood frame for the canopy and fit it with curtain rods, you will find it as easy to take the canopy down for laundering as you would ordinary curtains. If the fabric is of the permanent-press type, you will not mind frequent washing to keep it always fresh and appealingly dainty.

An atmosphere of quiet elegance pervades the master bed- ▶ room pictured across the page. It reflects the owners' fondness for antique furnishings, the patina of aged wood, and the historic patterns that were favorites of our colonial ancestors.

The old splat-back chairs and table form an inviting setting for morning coffee in this tranquil suite. The seat covers on the chairs are the solo touch of a brighter color.

The actual cost of this canopy treatment with the luxury look was just $75! A single mattress and box spring were transformed by adding a canopy made from ½-inch plywood cut the same size as the mattress and upholstered in felt.

The canopy was anchored in place with four 2-inch dowels screwed into the frame of the box spring. For a touch of glamour, three rope strands were wound around and glued to the dowels. A coat of shocking pink paint and a plaid coverlet in harmonizing colors added the finishing touches. The cost included plywood and dowels, felt, plaid fabric for the spread, cushions, and rope trim.

The nearby wall lamp makes this a favorite spot for study and leisure reading. The wall support for the lamp as well as its shade were given a color trim to coordinate with the overall red-pink scheme.

How To Decorate Difficult Areas Without Straining Your Budget

When you remodel your basement, attic, attached garage, or porch to gain additional living space, you are often faced with the problem of hiding unsightly walls. One solution is to use canvas panels. Simple to install and easy to care for, they are far less expensive than wood paneling and more durable than most other cloths.

Use inexpensive canvas panels to add a decorator touch to your recreation area.

"See if you can convert space you already have," is the best of advice to any family that feels cramped and is considering moving or building on extra rooms.

Basements and attics often offer a solution to the need for an extra room. An attached garage can sometimes be converted into a family or teen-age entertaining center; however, it will usually involve the more expensive step of providing added heating, which is seldom necessary in remodeling a basement or an attic.

The picture opposite shows just a corner of a sizable basement remodeling undertaken primarily to provide the younger members of the family with space for their own leisure use and for entertaining friends. It looks glamorous and expensive, but you really couldn't find a cheaper or less complicated way of reclaiming unused basement space for everyday living.

For such a project, the first steps are careful measuring and planning. You'll need an accurate floor plan drawn to scale (let ½ inch equal 1 foot of actual space) and indicating all walls, standing pipes, structural supports, and so on. In this case, the homeowners screened off the utility, storage, and laundry areas and divided the remaining space into two definite sections: one for a hobby and game center and one for television viewing. No architectural changes were necessary.

The next step was to paint walls, ceiling, and floor. (A rented sprayer speeds up this job.) All surfaces were painted a medium shade of gray—a good color for masking rough surfaces, odd shapes or angles. The floor was given a second coat of light speckle, and inexpensive carpeting was laid in the television corner. Since carpeting took the place of some seating (for those who like to sit or lie on the floor while watching television), it was both practical and economical.

Canvas is available in a wide range of colors, so you can follow any scheme you choose. Tent and awning companies will make panels to your measurements and install grommets that let you lace them to support poles. If you are looking for ways to keep costs at a bare minimum, you can do the sewing yourself and rent a machine to attach grommets.

It is best to buy canvas that has been treated to resist mildew, shrinking, and stretching, especially if your room has even the slightest tendency to be damp. To keep the canvas bright and new-looking requires only a periodic wipe with a damp sponge.

Carpentry required is minimal. The first step is to nail a 2 × 2 to the sill plate; next, nail a 2 × 4 across joists. These will act as braces at the top for the brass spring-tension poles onto which the canvas panels are to be laced and held taut.

For step-by-step directions in installation, see the pictures and captions on the following pages.

If you're interested in a space conversion project of the kind pictured here but your house has no basement or one that cannot be converted in this manner, consider converting your attic or a porch or attached garage. If you can possibly utilize space you already have, the cost of making it suitable to leisure-time uses will be a tiny fraction of the sum you'd need in order to add a new room at the ground level of your house.

But before planning to convert available space around your home, you should analyze it carefully to determine the amount of useful space it can provide. You may wish to call in an architect or a reputable building contractor to help you with this evaluation.

He will also be able to determine important structural requirements: Is the floor of the attic or porch strong enough to support any increased weight your project will add? Will a dormer be needed to provide headroom in an attic? Are basement floor and walls in good enough condition?

The inviting television and refreshment area at left bears little resemblance to what was formerly catchall basement space. Imaginative touches have helped develop a circus theme by modifying and camouflaging unsightly and obtrusive basement fixtures, thus making a virtue of necessity.

In the corner pictured, a fiber glass giraffe has turned an unsightly but essential pipe into an amusing decoration.

Window wells, such as the one just in back of the little girl in the picture, have become cages for a menagerie of stuffed circus animals. Ordinary wooden dowels were painted black and installed to resemble the bars on cages. Hand-painted frames for the "cages" bear the names of the animals housed in each—Leo and Tiny the Lions in one, Titan the Tiger in another of the converted window wells.

Pleated canvas curtains along the wall at the right of the giraffe screen off part of the utility and storage areas, yet leave them entirely accessible.

A refreshment bar was built of plywood, and canvas was applied to its curving base; plastic laminate on top is easy to wipe clean. Upended nail kegs with cushions that pivot make unusual stools.

The straight canvas panels used to cover most of the wall space are laced into place with stout cotton cord through grommets and around standard 1 1/2-inch diameter poles. Canvas panels are tacked at the top onto a wood support. A canvas valance covers this strip of wood and gives a neat top finish.

When installing a canopy ceiling of this kind, check first to see where the hanging loops will do the best job of camouflage to hide unattractive heating ducts or support beams. Then attach curtain rods at the strategic points and drape canvas over them.

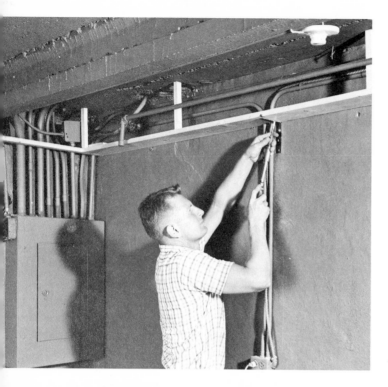

Your little theater has a wonderful all-purpose piece of scenery called a flat that can be easily transplanted to your home for decorating purposes. A flat is really a panel of canvas stretched tight to cover a wooden frame and glued and stapled to the frame's edges. This simple structure can be made in many sizes and has been used by centuries of stage designers to duplicate everything from castles in the air to train cabooses. In addition to being cheap and lightweight, the advantage of flats or canvas panels is a flat blank surface that can be painted to suit any decorating scheme.

When you are making a canvas panel at home, do not build the frame so tall or so wide

Basement remodeling, which may involve installing new floors, ceilings, or walls, is often an undertaking too time-consuming and too costly to consider. A good substitute for such extensive remodeling is the imaginative use of colored canvas panels, which can hide unsightly basement walls. Since canvas is available in a wide range of decorative colors and designs, the sky is the limit in choosing a decorative scheme. The canvas used here is a painted, 10-ounce, outdoor type in 31-inch width. The first step is to measure your basement. Then sketch a floor plan to help determine how to divide the basement space. Next, paint the walls, floors, and ceilings. Once you have completed these initial steps, you are ready to start installing the canvas. As shown in the top left picture, nail on the walls parallel to the joists a 2 x 2-foot board to the sill plate. Next, nail a 2 x 4 board across the joists, which then brace the poles at the top.

The next major step is no more complicated than the first. As shown in bottom picture, left, the standard 1-1/2-inch diameter poles are pushed into place 1 or 2 inches away from the wall. These poles are available at most building supply stores or departments. If you prefer, you can easily make your own poles using doweling 1-1/2 to 2 inches by 6-1/2 feet. Once the poles have been installed, the canvas should be tacked at the top and then laced into place with cotton cord. It is important to make sure that you interlace the loops and pull them taut. If this is not done, the canvas panels will sag and the decorative effects of the canvas will be lost. Canvas strips will fill the corners. Trim for windows and doorways can be planned by placing poles on either side of the opening. Notice that in the picture the homeowner has left one section uncovered by canvas. Later, he can decorate this space with a large stuffed animal, a favorite piece of sculpture, or a colorful decoration painted on the wall itself.

that the canvas will buckle. Six feet by four feet is a good size. Use 1 × 3s for the rectangular frame. Reinforce this frame at the corners with triangular pieces of plywood, and a 1 × 3-inch bar placed just above the center of the frame. Square the edges. Stretch the canvas tightly across the frame and, using a staple gun, staple the canvas to the frame's edges. Glue can be used as an extra reinforcement that will keep the canvas edges from fraying. One or both sides of the frame can be covered, and the edges masked. Use fireproof, presized canvas. When the panels are finished they can be painted with freehand designs, using thinned oil or water-base paint. Never use paint with a heavy vehicle that will buckle the canvas. If you have no talent for drawing or painting, use stenciled designs cut from

heavy paper with a single-edged razor. You can use folk-art motifs or designs copied from books. Paint them directly on the canvas, or spatter them on with a toothbrush. Best of all are the abstract splash paintings that you and the children can make in the backyard using liquid, nonanaline dyes. Stand several feet from the panel and throw or drop the color on the canvas for a colorful modern effect.

Once painted, canvas panels can be used in many ways. Nailed to a batten at the top and bottom, several of them form a false ceiling that can be hung to mask the real basement ceiling. Three or four panels hinged together make an unusual lightweight screen. Larger panels can be fitted into floor or ceiling tracks, with an occasional upright support, to create Japanese-style sliding room dividers or walls.

The picture below shows the last steps to be completed when decorating your basement with canvas panels. To finish your basement ceiling, loop the canvas through regular curtain rods fastened to the floor joists. Then tack the ends of the canvas curtain panels to the sill plate with a wooden strip. Plan it so that the loops will cover your heating ducts or supporting beams wherever possible, thus disguising these unsightly problems without a complicated or expensive remodeling job. For the finishing touch, tack up valances. Canvas is treated to resist mildew and will not expand or contract. Periodic sponging will keep it looking bright and new.

Here is an example of what to do with uncovered window wells. Let your window house a menagerie of wild (but stuffed) animals caged behind ordinary wooden dowels painted jailhouse black. Personalize the cage animals by painting wagon signs with their names: Titan the Tiger, Leo the Lion. In the picture, the homeowner also painted the cage with swirling areas of color. In the other window well he placed an electric man, elephant table, calliope, peep-show sign, and a giraffe. Thus, with colorful canvas, brass spring-tension poles, curtain rods, and a little thought, this home decorator created a circus-like atmosphere in his own home.

What You Must Know About Quality And Value In Floor Coverings

What is new in carpets and rugs? Just about everything, as you will see when you study the pictures here and on the pages that follow. Today more than ever before, you stand an excellent chance of getting a serviceable carpet or rug you'll enjoy for years at a price you can easily afford. But before you go shopping, decide what you really want and need in the way of color, texture, design, and quality.

Is wall-to-wall carpeting what you want? Or would a room-size rug better meet your requirements? You can use either—or more likely, both—in your home. It's a matter of what effect you want and how the particular room is to be used.

Wall-to-wall carpeting covers the floor completely and has the ability to make any room seem larger because of the unifying effect of unbroken color and texture. A room cut up by architectural jogs will probably benefit from the wall-to-wall treatment.

Rugs are available in prefinished standard sizes, such as 9 × 12 or 12 × 15 feet, or they can be cut to size from rolls of carpet. *Broadloom* is simply a term of measurement for any carpeting wider than 6 feet. It doesn't define a particular quality or type of construction. Room-size rugs generally leave a border around a room—about 8 inches from the wall in a small room, 10 to 12 inches in larger one. In rooms with standard proportions (12 × 15, for example) a room-size rug can cover the floor completely just as installed wall-to-wall carpeting does.

Choose appearance first when buying rugs or carpeting. Floor covering is a major factor in your decorating scheme, and unless you like its effect, the performance and price will seem unimportant.

Also consider the practical aspects of color and texture. If you want a minimum of carpet maintenance, choose a color that does not show soil readily—medium, rather than very light or very dark, shades; color mixtures; tweeds or multicolor patterns. In heavy-traffic areas such as the living room, family room, or hallway, you'll want carpets that don't show every footprint. So look for tight, dense textures, such as twists, loops, or textured surfaces that combine cut and looped yarns.

Today's carpets and rugs come in an overwhelming variety of colors. To simplify the selection process, think in terms of "color families"—blue, green, red, gold, beige, or brown. Then look for variations within that group—the exact shade of gold or green you want, or a practical tweedy mixture.

Many stores offer "in-home shopping" that helps you make the best selection. It is wise to visit the store first, however, for a broad look at all of the possible choices; then narrow the field to a few favorite colors. Take samples home and study them in relation to your own particular furnishings and lighting.

Do not feel you must settle for a "safe neutral." Although vivid colors may seem too bold, they can often be toned down by other furnishings in the room. Carpeting with a strong pattern may appear limiting at first, but its "built-in" color scheme may be a valuable guide in choosing other furnishings and accessories.

How to judge pile

Remember the phrase "the deeper, the denser, the better." This refers to the surface pile (sometimes called "face yarns"), which takes the brunt of hard wear. Dense pile, with tufts closely packed together, wears the longest because the yarns help to support each other and resist both bending and abrasion.

Surface pile today may be made of natural or man-made fibers. The type of fiber used is not, by itself, a guarantee of quality or performance. However, various fibers do have their own characteristics that affect style, performance, or economy.

Since many fibers are often referred to by their trade names rather than their generic type, it will be helpful to familiarize yourself with the table at right and the information it contains about important man-made fibers used in the manufacture of rugs and carpeting. See the following pages for additional buymanship pointers.

Deep-pile carpeting in a golden-beige tone provides a pleasing background for the large-scale upholstered furniture pieces that have been chosen for their comfort as well as their contemporary design. The neutral tone of the wall-to-wall carpet gives an expansive appearance to this large room. This expansiveness is further emphasized by the same neutral tone on the walls. By leaving the floor and wall areas subdued, the individual furniture pieces are allowed to stand out. This is especially true of the massive coffee table with its rounded corners and curved apron and legs that is in sharp contrast to the rest of the room's furnishings.

With a neutral background, you can splash color about the room by using bright, bold colors in the accessories. Note the leopard print pillows on the sofa and the yellow flowers.

FIBERS AND TRADE NAMES

ACRYLIC
Acrilan (The Chemstrand Company)
Creslan (American Cyanamid Company)
Orlon 33 (E. I. DuPont deNemours & Company, Inc.)
Zefran (Dow Badische)
Zefkrome (Dow Badische)

BI-CONSTITUENT
Source (Allied Chemical Corporation)

MODACRYLIC
Dynel (Union Carbide Corporation)
Verel (Eastman Chemical Products, Inc.)

NYLON
Anso (Allied Chemical Corporation)
Antron (E. I. DuPont deNemours & Company, Inc.)
Caprolan (Allied Chemical Corporation)
Cumuloft (The Chemstrand Company)
DuPont (E. I. DuPont deNemours & Company, Inc.)
  (Note: "501" is a DuPont certification mark)
Enkaloft (American Enka Corp.)
Tycora (Textured Yarn Company)

POLYESTER
Fortrel (Celanese Corp.)
Kodel (Eastman Chemical Products, Inc.)
Vycron (Beaunit)

POLYPROPYLENE OLEFIN
Herculon (Hercules Powder Company)
Marvess (Alamo Industries)
Polycrest (UniRoyal)
Vectra (The Vectra Company)

RAYON
Avicron (American Viscose)
Avisco (American Viscose)
Coloray (Courtaulds)

Types of fibers

Characteristics of fibers

Wool is the classic fiber for carpets, and it offers these desirable characteristics: resiliency, abrasion-resistance, adaptability to styling, warmth and comfort to touch, and soil-resistance. By reason of these qualities, wool often serves as a "yardstick" when judging other fibers used in rugs and carpets.

All-wool and wool-blend carpets now manufactured by major companies are permanently mothproofed during the manufacturing process. Check for this feature on labels.

The man-made fibers especially engineered for carpet use are the *acrylics* and *modacrylics, nylon, polypropylene, olefin,* and *rayon.* These are the generic types of fibers, and they must be clearly specified on carpet labels or invoices, although the trade name (see table on preceding page) may also be used in labeling a carpet.

The *acrylics* and their close cousins, the *modacrylics,* strongly resemble wool in resiliency, abrasion-resistance, softness, and warmth. Like all man-made fibers, they are mildew-resistant, naturally mothproof, and easily adaptable to styling since they can be controlled for uniformity in production.

Nylon is especially noted for abrasion-resistance. It is a "smooth" fiber that will resist water-absorption so that stains soluble in water may be easily removed. The fiber is used in two forms—staple nylon, seen most frequently in cut-pile textures, and continuous-filament nylon, developed to eliminate the tendency to fuzzing and pilling.

Polypropylene and *polyester* are the most recent fibers developed for carpet use. In appearance, polypropylene is similar to a continuous-filament nylon. It is also noted for its abrasion- and soil-resistance. Polyester is a strong, durable, and resilient fiber that resists abrasion, sunlight, chemicals, insects, mold, and mildew.

In many modern homes, an open architectural style that eliminates all or a large part of certain walls gives a larger decorating role to carpets than was previously the case.

Here, at left, partial separation of space by means of a dramatically soaring half-wall of exposed brick presents a real challenge for the decorator. In a blue-green scheme, broadloom carpeting cut to appropriate size and shape is laid on a hard-surface flooring of green, and the identical floor treatment is carried into the partly visible room beyond. Heavy traffic between the two areas will be via the hard-surface area of the floor, reducing the problems of maintenance and wear that would exist if the pale blue carpeting were used throughout both rooms. In this arrangement a medium-priced carpet should be a satisfactory choice.

Textural interest is one of the most important contributions that can be made ▶ by carpets and rugs to the overall decoration of a room. In addition to increasing comfort and helping to absorb sound, soft floor coverings provide a textural counterpoint for the sleek surface of woods used in furniture, flat fabrics, and wall coverings with sheen.

New types of rugs and carpets on the market range from those with velvety soft piles to shaggy ones with a hand-crafted look. Some, such as the one at right, combine high-cut and low pile, lending a pleasantly informal air to the decor.

The rugs and carpets called shags are particularly effective in combination with country and provincial furnishings; their rough textures are a nice complement to the sturdy lines of chairs, tables, sofas.

In a room furnished in a style similar to this one, with patterned wall covering and matching draperies, patterned upholstery, and colorful accent pieces, a carpet of a neutral shade is the most tasteful choice.

Rayon and *cotton* provide added choices in economical carpets and rugs. A relatively small percentage of these fibers is used as the sole agent in carpet production today; however, both are used in the manufacture of rugs. These fibers crush rather easily—a characteristic that can be minimized by density of construction—but they can be used to good advantage in low traffic areas, and their styling possibilities are good.

Carpets may also be made of fiber blends. In blending natural or man-made fibers today, manufacturers use the same technique employed for blending wool—choosing one grade for luster, another for toughness—to take advantage of several fiber traits.

For example, when wool is reinforced by nylon in a 70 to 30 ratio, the finished carpet looks and feels most like its predominant fiber—wool. Generally, at least 20 percent of a fiber must be used in the blend before it makes any noticeable contribution to the finished product.

Testing for quality

Use your eyes and your hands; holding a sample of the carpet, bend it between your fingers until you can see the closeness of construction. The less backing you can see, the denser (and longer wearing) is the pile. If you are able to see a strip of backing and the pile is lower, less densely tufted, the quality of the carpet will also be poorer.

In deciding on the quality you will choose, consider what sort of use the carpet will receive. It will prove worth the expense to select top quality for heavy-traffic areas. Medium quality will serve well for average use, and budget quality for light use. These are guideposts you should follow in carpet selection.

You don't actually have to count footsteps to measure traffic in your home; just be realistic about the types of activity and the degree of wear your carpet will be subjected to in normal, everyday use. Remember, too, that it is poor economy to buy carpet that has to be replaced in a few years.

Price ranges are also a clue to quality. A carpet in the economy range, roughly from $5.95 to $8.95 per square yard, should serve you well in a light-traffic area such as a guest room, or last a shorter time if given normal daily use. A medium-priced carpet, $9.95 to $12.95 per square yard, is suitable for many home areas, including bedrooms, dining room, and living room.

Top quality is essential in heavy-traffic areas, including living rooms that double as family rooms, and stairs and hallways used daily by members of the family.

To get full value, always select wall-to-wall carpeting from a middle price range upward. A good room-sized rug, which can be turned to equalize the wear, is a better buy than a cheap grade of wall-to-wall carpeting.

Some manufacturers produce three price grades of carpet with identical texture and color. In this way you can get matching carpet throughout your home at less cost.

Construction and care

Construction as well as fiber content and appearance enter into the price of carpeting, and a certain amount of cost also goes into the backing. For every dollar over that figure, you are paying for surface pile. The more pile, the more expensive the carpeting and the longer it will wear. This explains why two carpets or rugs that look very much alike and are made of the same fiber can have widely differing price tags.

Carpets may be woven, tufted, or knitted—the method used should not be a source of confusion. Manufacturers use all three methods to achieve varying styles and qualities, and one type is not necessarily better than another one of the group.

In weaving and knitting, surface yarns and pile yarns are interlocked at the same time. Principal types of weaves are Wilton, Axminster, and velvet; these are not brand names, but names for types of looms.

In tufting, surface yarns are attached to a preconstructed backing. On all tufted and knitted carpets, the backing is coated with latex for security of surface yarns. Most good-quality tufted carpets also have an extra layer of backing fabric laminated to the primary backing for greater strength.

The advantages of padding

Padding is essential to good carpet installation. Also called "cushioning" or "underlay," it should also be used under larger rugs. Most important of all on rough and uneven floors, it prolongs carpet life as well as adding to comfort underfoot.

The most popular types of padding are felted cushioning, made of 100 percent hair or a combination of hair and jute, and rubber cushioning, either foam or sponge.

Another type of cushion, felted hair with a rubber coating, combines the desirable features of both types, since the rubber coating keeps out dust and dirt that collect in hair and jute padding. Foam cushions are not as long-lasting as those of sponge rubber, which are also the springiest.

Whichever type you select, choose a good quality rather than a cheaper one. Expect to pay from $1.25 to $2.50 per square yard, depending upon the thickness and weight.

Take good care of your carpeting

Proper care can greatly extend the life of carpeting and rugs. By giving them regular upkeep and attention—a thorough vacuuming (about seven slow, careful strokes over each section) at least once a week—you will prevent most dirt particles from becoming embedded into the base of the tufts and cutting the fibers.

Spills and stains should be removed immediately. You will avoid much permanent damage if you remove spills and stains before they dry and become embedded. For this reason it is a good idea to keep two household cleaning aids—the dry-cleaning fluid you use to remove spots from clothing, and a detergent-vinegar-water solution—always on hand. To prepare the second solution, simply add a teaspoonful of mild detergent and a teaspoonful of vinegar to a quart of water.

Remove butter, grease, ball-point ink, and other oils by first wiping off excess material, then applying the dry-cleaning fluid. Use as much dry cleaner as necessary, then dry the carpet and lightly brush up the pile.

You need both dry-cleaning fluid and the detergent solution to remove stains caused by milk, eggs, salad dressing, and ice cream, and the special stains of coffee, chocolate, blood, and vomit. After blotting up surface liquid, apply detergent solution. Dry the carpet, then apply dry-cleaning fluid. Dry the carpet again and brush the pile into place.

In all treatments, make sure the carpet does not become too wet or remain wet too long.

Fuzz, uneven tufts, and shading are often sources of worry when carpeting is new. None is serious. If you have new carpeting, expect it to fuzz or shed for several months. The pilling effect is due to initial wear and tear on new fibers. Exposure to use and the resulting friction cause the end strands to ball up. It is a natural condition and has no effect on the life of the carpet. Just use a vacuum cleaner lightly each day to keep the carpet looking neat until it stops shedding.

High heels may create another problem. If they pull or snag loop pile or thick, long-tufted carpeting, you will have uneven tufts. You can easily remove them by snipping them down to make them even with the surface.

At other times, you may notice a change in the color tone of your carpet. This is known as shading, and it occurs when tufts have been pressed in different directions by footsteps or the weight of furniture.

You can make shading less noticeable by vacuuming only in the direction of the pile. If you are not sure which direction is correct, run your finger over the surface—a smooth feeling shows the direction of the pile.

Crush marks caused by weight of furniture can be treated by placing a damp cloth over a hot iron and holding the iron briefly above the spot. Or hold a heated steam iron about a half inch above the spot for a minute. Be sure you *steam,* don't *iron* the carpet.

Vibrant, clear colors and a new range of neutrals offer the carpet shopper a greater variety than ever before. Advancing colors such as the red wall-to-wall carpeting in this room can key an entire color scheme. Notice, too, how the same soft floor covering runs up the stairs and onto an entry hall balcony to relate the two areas.

Earthy colors of upholstery and accessories subtly blend with the carpeting without lessening its impact. Should you decide to use a strong color on one of your floors, you will be wise to temper it with areas of neutralizing black and white, and with wood colors as has been done here.

Carpeting should be chosen as carefully as a jeweler selects a choice stone. If it is well chosen, your furnishings are shown to advantage; if not, their beauty is dimmed. Carpeting, which is essentially background, reflects your overall decorating mood.

Suggestions For Building With An Eye Toward Later Conversion

The carport has gained importance as an attractive and economical solution to automobile storage. And when it is also designed to house garden tools, games, and sports equipment, it is an even more desirable home-improvement project.

For owners of older homes who have taken advantage of attached garages as a way to expand living space, the carport can also be the smart replacement after such a remodeling project.

If the man of the family is a skilled carpenter and has successfully handled other comparable building projects, he may consider doing much of the carport construction himself. But certain steps—roof construction, for example—require the cooperation of at least two persons, and you may decide to hire a contractor to do the job.

The basic elements of most carports are a poured concrete floor and a roof supported by four or more posts. A worthwhile extra is a storage cabinet, as in the carport pictured on the opposite page.

If you plan to have the carport built, it is wise to make some rough sketches of exactly what you want before calling on a contractor for an estimate. The ideal way to get comparable bids from several contractors is to have an architect draw up plans and specifications. The charge should be about 10 to 12 percent of the job cost. If the architect follows through with construction supervision, his fee may run between 12 and 15 percent of total construction costs.

If you feel that a job such as this is not large enough to warrant engaging an archi-tect, you should at least try to select the general types of materials you want used. Study the examples pictured here. (See also *Architecture,* Vol. 2.)

Keep in mind the style of architecture of your house and the materials of which it is built. A carport will be most attractive if it is in harmony with your home.

If yours is an older home of brick, for instance, you probably would not want a carport of natural redwood. Instead, you might paint it to match the color of your house trim, keep it simple in lines, and roof it in the same manner as that of your house.

When you have decided on style, materials, dimensions, and other details, ask two or three contractors to make bids. (More than three tend to confuse the picture.) If possible, get bids from contractors whose work has proved satisfactory to your friends and neighbors. Make a point of looking at comparable examples of their work elsewhere in your vicinity. You might also inquire of your bank about the contractors' financial standing.

When talking with a contractor, make sure: (1) that the estimate will state the full price for the job and the approximate length of time the contractor will take to do it; (2) that the contractor carries workmen's compensation and liability insurance; and (3) if he is given the job, that he will prepare a written contract that will contain all plans and exact specifications for the work to be done.

If you already have a carport but it is not equipped with storage cabinets, consider adding such space as convenient housing for the lawnmower and various other pieces of gar-

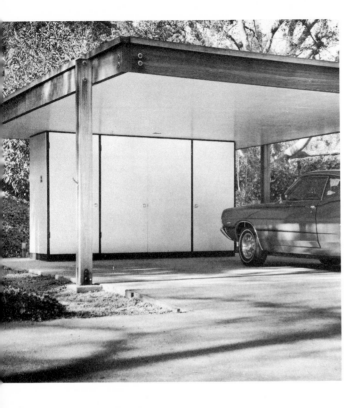

den equipment, for outdoor furniture, barbecue grill, sport and game equipment, bicycles, tricycles, and so on.

The best way to decide upon the size and space divisions needed in such a storage cabinet is to assemble all of the items you'll want to house. Measure to see how much space all the large items require. Consider the possibility that fitting one section of the cabinet with shelves would make it better suited to your needs. (See *Cabinets,* p. 676.)

An inexpensive family room

Look first to carport or garage if you have space problems and are considering adding a room to your house. Use of the existing roof

A carport should be just as up-to-date as the new car you park in it. There is no reason at all, as the attractive structure pictured here indicates. Large enough to store two standard cars easily, it also has room to park anything else, from bicycles to motorcycles. You may want to include a compact workshop in the storage section at the rear of the carport, which is divided into three sections for maximum convenience and efficiency.

The simple, flat roof is supported by 5x6-inch posts. The underside of the roof was finished with plywood and painted white to make the interior seem even more open. Placing the posts outside the slab minimizes the chance of scraping a fender. If your lot does not have this much space available, the same plan can be adapted to a one-car version.

The posts and fascia are of natural redwood; black trim outlines the triple storage center. Style and colors were chosen to harmonize with the modern house; other wood finishes are possible for carports, in harmony with the color and style of older vintage houses.

The storage area at the back of this carport is organized in three sections, with two large doors opening up the center section to receive bicycles and other bulky pieces. For your family this might be the place to house the portable grill, folding outdoor furniture, etc.

The cabinet at left has shelves for storing paint, garden tools, car needs; the right-hand cabinet is compartmented for convenient housing of large garden equipment (mower, spreader, leaf sweeper, and so on). Since all space is flexible, you can work out the division that best suits your needs.

If your lot is so arranged that locating a storage unit at the back of the carport is convenient, this style will interest you. But it is not necessary to place the unit in this fashion if another arrangement (at one of the sides, for example) would be more convenient. The rule is to place the storage unit where it will save you the most steps.

Landscaping is an important, but often neglected, part of remodeling projects that involve an addition to a house. By skillful placement of the right trees, vines, and shrubs, it is often possible to camouflage differences in color between the building material of the original structure and the addition.

To blend an addition into the landscape, choose plants and shrubs with regard to exposure. Place plants that need sun on the south or west side, and those liking shade on the east or north. Take care that the roof overhang does not shield the plants from rain.

and foundation will greatly reduce your construction costs. The style and materials used in building will match or be in good harmony with those of your house, helping to ensure that the addition will not conflict with the basic architectural design.

In the case of the well-handled remodeling project pictured and described on this and the facing page, a former carport was enclosed with brick to match the main building material of the house proper. So skillfully handled was the execution that not a hint of the former use remains in the new family room that has been gained.

The shake roof, compatible with rough brick, is the one that originally covered the carport. A doorway in the new end wall saves traffic through the house, permits direct entry.

Interior construction in the new family room sustains the architectural flavor of the exterior, is practically damageproof, requires minimal maintenance. The brick floor takes

The floor plan below shows how the original design of the carport placed this area in relation to the house, at an angle that left a triangular space between it and the kitchen entrance; this space had been used to house the washing machine and hot-water heater.

Generous dimensions (20 × 24 feet) made the carport suitable for conversion to a spacious family room. The tool storage unit along one wall of the carport lent itself nicely to reuse for storage and utility.

Moving the former utility area allows the kitchen and family rooms to adjoin each other and facilitates the serving of meals or refreshments in the family room.

In the photograph opposite, you see how a counter and pass-through with louvered shutters can close off the kitchen view when that is desired.

The kitchen, too, has benefited from the remodeling, gaining enough space to permit installation of added cabinets and a table for family meals.

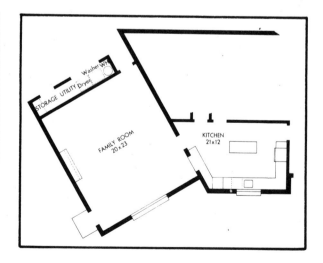

the heaviest kind of wear, and the shutters reduce the need for draperies or curtains that require cleaning or laundry.

The plank-and-beam ceiling is in keeping with a decor that relies for its appeal primarily on contrasting textures: smooth polished wood against the roughness of a brick floor and walls of exposed brick.

Furnishings follow architecture to create a warm, inviting, but casual mood. The Hitchcock-style chairs cushioned in colorful fabric of a small-printed pattern, the simple round table and accompanying lazy Susan, the period light fixture suspended from the ceiling, all are keyed to the design of the room.

Also suitable in this setting would have been furnishings and fabrics of either the French or Italian provincial styles; sturdy indoor-outdoor carpeting might have been used in place of the brick floor.

Carport conversion

A simple conversion netted this family a western-style family room of generous proportions,

Exposed adobe brick, which forms two of the inner walls of the new family room, has an attractive regional flavor suitable to the Southwestern architectural style of the house. Furnishings of Early American design (excellent reproductions as well as antiques are now on the market) increase the inviting, casual mood and suit the informality that permits heavy use of the room without concern over upkeep.

An interesting window treatment is important in a room as simply furnished as this one, relying as it does on little but nature's colors (brick and wood) for decorative effect.

Use of wood shutters of a natural finish for the lower half of the one large window solves the problem of long draperies that could be in the way of active games. Café curtains of a nubby fabric inject color.

The original house, built of adobe brick and cedar and roofed with clay tiles, was aesthetically well suited to its location in the low mountains of Arizona. Borrowing from hacienda architecture, the house was given privacy at the front by a low wall of the same adobe brick, topped with tiles.

The wide expanse of the carport, pictured above as it looked before remodeling, was open at both ends so that cars could drive on through a turnaround at the rear of the house (now reached from a newly located entrance).

The low lines of house and carport make the structure seem to nestle comfortably into its picturesque landscape. Earth colors of brick and tile strengthen its basic kinship with the setting.

The skillful handling of the remodeling project has left intact the architect's original conception of unity between the house and its unusual setting. Cedar panels that fill in the carport roof line blend well with the color of burned adobe brick used for the house and wall.

The panel of horizontal cedar boards installed at windowsill level across the lower front portion of the converted carport helps to maintain the attractive low lines of the total structure. A driveway that formerly led into the carport has been resurfaced and now serves as parking for guests' cars.

The container-grown plant at left and the low rock border protecting the new mound planted with groundcover reinforce the unified appearance of the family-room addition and the main part of the house.

a room to be enjoyed by all members of the family and their guests.

The photograph at left shows the location of the original carport in relation to the rest of the house. Its roof lines made simple the task of relating it to the primary architectural style when it was changed from its essential "lean-to" character to become an integral part of the whole.

Pictured at the bottom of the page is an exterior view of the new family room; interior views are shown on the facing page. As the exterior view reveals, no structural changes were required in order to create the new living space—merely the enclosing of the front and rear of the carport.

Architectural unity, offering guide lines for interior decoration, prevents the new room from appearing "tacked on" to the original structure. If you are buying or building a new home but expect to need more space later than that afforded by the house at present, look for possibilities of expansion such as those that obviously existed from the beginning in this case.

Continuous roof lines and use of building materials that are identical or well related to those of the house itself are probably the two most important factors involved in giving an addition the appearance of "belonging." Nothing reveals more quickly—or more unattractively—that an addition is an afterthought than conflicting styles or unmatched building materials used in the roof or siding of the addition.

Landscape plantings, too, can help link the house proper and whatever addition you may choose to make to it. Indeed, a new addition to your home provides a chance to relandscape your whole yard, and building scars can be covered with quick-growing varieties of vines and trees. A strategically placed tree or group of shrubs can dramatically improve the relationship between the house proper and an additional room.

Exposed beams and decking of the ceiling pictured above remain unchanged in this carport conversion project. The existing concrete floor of the carport needed only thorough cleaning and waxing to become suitable for the new room, with accent rugs placed to emphasize furniture groupings.

In a room whose dominant features are an interesting wood ceiling and exposed adobe brick wall, furnishings are appropriately simple and masculine in character.

Comfortable couches offer good seating when the room is used by family or for entertaining; they convert to beds when the room accommodates guests—for which it is well suited, since there are no direct connections with other living areas.

Other guestroom features are the closet, whose door is visible at left in the picture below, and a small bathroom, which was installed in the former carport storage space at the front of the house near the door to the terrace (see photo at bottom of opposite page to identify the location of this space).

In a mountain area where sunlight is often intense, roll-down blinds admit filtered light. They are supplemented by draw draperies to give nighttime privacy when the room serves as a guest room.

Large windows take advantage of the interest of the surrounding terrain, and a high-power telescope on a tripod permits observation of distant birds and other wildlife.

CASUAL FURNISHINGS

Bring The Outdoors Indoors With Casual Furnishings

The rigid line that formerly was drawn between furniture suitable for outdoor use and that used inside a home no longer exists. Today's indoor scene often relies on furniture fashioned of materials and styled along lines that once would have marked it as porch furniture only. Even if there is really nothing new under the sun, it is certainly new in feeling to decorate one's living room with casual furnishings patterned after outdoor pieces.

Especially attractive to young homemakers are the high-style lines of furniture made of wicker, metal, rattan, plastics, and all the other carefree materials that are relatively low in cost but high in casual appeal. Furniture of this sort may be purchased out of fairly skimpy budgets, and later be used in a family room—or outdoors—when increased income and a move to larger quarters bring changes in living.

The well-established family, too, will find attraction in the latest furniture made of metal or fibers and upholstered in easily-cared-for man-made plastics. Such pieces are ideal candidates for family-room furnishings, for recreation rooms to be used by the younger generation, and for the multipurpose room that sometimes doubles as a guest room.

Brilliant colors that involve no cleaning problems are one of the major attractions of the vinyls used to upholster many pieces, such as those pictured in both of the rooms shown here. Pastels and vivid hues alike wipe clean with a damp sponge, and can take steady use over long periods of time without showing signs of wear.

Take your color cues from a painting as this room does. The procedure is usually foolproof, since the artist has already decided for you what colors to emphasize and what amounts you should use.

With modern synthetics and casual furniture styles, you can feel free to use this vivid palette with no worries about wear or cleaning. Floor coverings as well as upholstery materials are the beneficiaries of modern miracles in fibers and finishes.

Gone is the day when synthetics bore the connotation of "substitute," or "second best." Today we welcome a synthetic into our homes for what it is—a product of science, specifically made to do a particular job better. This new attitude toward synthetics results from steady improvement in quality, color, texture, and beauty, and in such attributes as durability and ease of care.

Today's furniture designers and interior decorators recognize the happy affinity between modern American and Scandinavian furniture and Oriental designs. In this room, twin mushroom-shaped footstools of wicker and a fancifully ornate hanging bird cage used as a plant container represent the Oriental influence. So, too, do the end tables of wood.

Modern in design, but repeating the use of wicker (with metal frames for sturdiness) are the attractive sofa and chairs. The ruby fabric that covers the sofa and one wall is thrown into focus and refreshingly cooled by curtains of sheer white that cover an entire wall of windows.

The black of the chair upholstery, hanging cage, and metal furniture frames offers a welcome contrast. A decorating trick worth noting: the injection of a small amount of black or near-black improves almost any decorating scheme.

Furniture such as this, here used in a family room, is an excellent example of the interesting new casual furniture on today's market—flexible as to use, simple to care for, relatively easy on the decorating budget.

New plastic spray-on coatings used by manufacturers of modern wicker furniture make it more durable than that found on grandmother's porch, and prevent its snagging clothing.

CEILINGS

New Ways To Dramatize Your Ceilings With Color, Pattern, Texture, And Light

Taking their inspiration from the handsome decorated ceilings of châteaus, castles, and stately country mansions, some of today's leading designers use out-of-the-ordinary ceiling treatments to call attention to the usually neglected "fifth wall." Wallpaper, fabrics, carpeting, cork, paneling, floor planking, luminous panels, and beams are used imaginatively to spotlight ceilings.

Architectural lines that include dormers, arches, slanting angles, and exposed beams lend themselves naturally to unique decorative ceiling treatments. But don't be disheartened if your room lacks such a feature to inspire your ingenuity. It can be just as exciting to transform an ordinary plastered ceiling with pattern, color, and texture to make it the stand-out feature of the decorating scheme.

Make the ceiling part of your decor

At one time ceilings were strictly functional constructions. Now, with the aid of new materials, ceilings can have decorative functions as well, and be suited to a particular furniture style.

Beams made of plastic, styrofoam, or plywood are lightweight and simple to install. Ornamented, they go well in a classic room; distressed, they fit into either a country-type or a contemporary room.

Floor planking used to cover ceilings can be tinted to carry out a basic color scheme, or finished in a natural wood tone. This type requires no maintenance and goes well with provincial styles of furnishings.

Luminous ceiling panels are effective with modern furnishings. They can be installed over the entire ceiling, or over just a part of it to highlight decorative accessories.

Concealed lighting behind coves can go with modern or traditional furnishings, depending on the design of the coving. (See *Built-in Lighting,* p. 656.)

Tips about beamed ceilings

Wood-beamed ceilings are a perennial favorite as a way to gain overhead drama. Today, with man-made beams of synthetics that look like hand-hewn wood beams, you don't have to worry about the extra structural weight that might rule out the installation of wood beams. You can buy boxlike vinyl beams that fasten to wood strips nailed to the ceiling, or lightweight plastic foam beams that you glue in place. Beams of urethane composition, for instance, weigh as little as 10 pounds per 20-foot beam—a fraction of the hundreds of pounds that wood of the same dimensions weighs. With either type, you have to touch the beams to tell them from the real thing. You can make your own beams from clear 1 × 4s or 1 × 6s. Attach these to wood strips on the ceiling and finish them with moldings to match the trim around windows and doors.

If you use dark woods, remember to balance them with ample light and bright hues. (See *Beamed Ceilings,* Vol. 3.)

This family room with its muted blue tones and outdoor ▶ feeling was constructed from a farmhouse porch. The original line of the porch is kept by a betasseled border panel that sections off the ceiling, makes it look lower, and gives the sofa area a feeling of formality and privacy that contrasts with the informality of the rest of the room.

Suspended ceiling systems are fast gaining in popularity. They are relatively inexpensive and can help you stretch that remodeling dollar. Although a suspended ceiling looks like a formidable undertaking, it is actually quite easy to install. A lightweight metal framework suspended from the ceiling joists—with a wall molding at the new ceiling height—supports the modular-size panels. To install, first determine the height of the new ceiling and mark this point by snapping a level chalk line around the perimeter of the room. Then, as shown above, attach the molding to the wall using the chalk line as a leveling guide.

Your next step in installing your suspended ceiling is to screw steel eyelets into the joists or existing ceiling at 4-foot intervals. After you have done this, attach the hanger wires to the eyelets. Then bend each of the wires at the point where they intersect the reference string you have put at 1⅛-inches above the wall molding. These reference (or leveling) strings should run along one short wall and one long wall of the room—set at the desired ceiling height. Installing a suspended ceiling doesn't call for a great amount of skill, but it is important that you take your time—particularly in these beginning steps—to measure accurately.

Now you are ready to install the first main runner. Do this by resting one end of the runner on the wall molding and then fastening the other end of the runner to the bent wire. Next, twist the wire several times to secure the loose end. Once this is done, you can start working your way back along the runner, fastening the hanger wires every four feet. By doing this, you can provide added support for the runners. Continue this procedure until all your main runners are installed and secured. Make sure your runners are low enough so when the tile is put in, unsightly wiring, pipes, and ductwork are covered up, and cracked, chipped ceilings are hidden.

The advantages of acoustical ceilings

Acoustical ceilings in their earliest form depended upon nothing more than the arrangement of perforations to deaden sound. Now there are endless decorating possibilities to be found in the variety of textures available.

The ceilings come in pebbly surfaces, swirls, or starbursts, and in warm neutral colors, some with metallic accents. As your color preferences change, the ceiling can be painted with flat oil-base paint, provided you avoid applying so much as to clog the acoustical perforations.

An acoustical ceiling, properly installed, absorbs between 55 and 75 percent of the sound waves striking it. This is an advantage in any room in the home that attracts family activity. It is especially helpful in the kitchen, which has so many noise-making appliances.

Essentially, acoustical ceilings are of three types: tile ceilings, plank ceilings, and suspended ceilings. All three are simple to install for anyone who is handy with tools. Just a few spare evenings, or a weekend, should be time enough to complete the job. If you elect to have a professional installation, your building-supply dealer may offer an installation service, or recommend someone who is competent to do the job.

Ceiling tiles, planks, and panels retain their new look for years. Some have a vinyl coating that resists grease. When cleaning becomes necessary, the ceiling can be wiped with a damp sponge without damaging the finish.

Suspended ceilings have gained acceptance in residential remodeling projects for a number of reasons. They offer an inexpensive way to lower old-fashioned high ceilings; to cover unsightly wiring, ducts, and pipes; and to conceal cracked and peeling ceilings. A lightweight metal framework suspended from the ceiling joists, with a wall molding at the new

By installing your ceiling lower than the ductwork, pipes, and other fixtures, you still reap the advantage of being able to get at any area of the ceiling quite easily. All you have to do once your ceiling is complete and the panels are in place is simply to lift out the ceiling panel to gain access. After you have completed the three steps given on the preceding page, you are now ready for step number four in the installation process. As shown in the top right picture, 4-foot cross T's are installed between the main runners you have secured. Place these cross T's at 24-inch intervals. This may vary if your ceiling panels are of a different size. Once the T's are placed, you can insert the end tab into the main runner slot. Then all you do is push it to lock. Your framework is complete and you now have a sturdy grid system.

As shown in the second picture on the right, you can now lay the ceiling panels into the grid. Your suspension system is complete. When putting the panels into the grid, tilt the panel edge slightly upward, as shown, then slide slowly through the opening. Work slowly and you won't break or chip off the edges of the ceiling tile. Once you negotiate the panel through the open grid, rest it on the grid flanges. Follow this procedure with the other tiles. Although you probably will use acoustical ceiling tile, there are other materials you may want to consider, such as wood paneling. To figure your ceiling's square footage, measure the width and length of the room, and then round off to the next full foot. Multiply these measurements and add the number of feet of the room's longest wall. This addition is for cutting and waste allowances. When shopping for ceiling panels, you will find a variety of textures, designs, colors, and materials from which to choose.

ceiling height, supports the modular-size panels. If you want no-glare lighting, you can install fluorescent lighting fixtures over luminous panels that can be incorporated into the ceiling grid system. If it is necessary to make repairs to the wiring, ducts, or pipes after the suspended ceiling is installed, they are easily accessible. Simply remove the proper panel to get at the problem area and replace it after the job is done.

Although installing a suspended ceiling looks like a formidable undertaking, it actually is rather easy. You have to use a little common sense when you cut the main frame members, but once this is done, the whole thing goes together very simply.

With one of the new suspended grid units that hang from the ceiling without touching the walls, you can put a new ceiling in your bathroom. The lighting is built in, including a sunlamp if you like.

◀ Striped paper in jewel tones is featured dramatically on the bathroom ceiling at left. Its colors are picked up and repeated by bath linens and other accessories. Keeping the walls off-white emphasizes the interest of the ceiling treatment.

In purchasing wallpaper for a bathroom, it is wise to select one that is water resistant or plastic coated. In any room that will often be damp, a water-sensitive paper would be a poor choice and uneconomical. Most treated papers may be wiped clean with a damp sponge; some can even withstand real scrubbing. Ask your dealer for cleaning recommendations.

In a high-ceilinged room, consider visually lowering one section of it by creating a gazebo effect such as the one pictured below. The first step is installation of a simple carpentry frame. Drape it with fabric to cover the lumber completely. A matching fabric is used to fashion the tie-back draperies and scalloped valance, as well as for a tailored tablecloth that falls clear to the floor.

This inviting and sophisticated dining area was originally the foyer of an apartment that lacked separate dining space. But the same idea could easily be adapted to separate one corner, or an alcove, of any large living room with equally stylish results.

The "big top" canopy shown in the sun porch above gives a look of carnival appearance when it is teamed with a flamboyant floral upholstery print. The canopy of cotton canvas was stapled to the wooden slatted ceiling. Nautical cotton cording neatly conceals the seams and is wound in a circle at the apex point. For a final decorative touch, upholstery fringe and oversize tassels outline the scalloped edges.

The total environment look of this dining area is created by the bright, flowered wallpaper on both walls and ceiling. The fresh garden motif in orange and yellow also outlines the white antique mirror with its cutaway, flower-embossed frame. The crisp orange and white floor, glass-topped table, and white chairs emphasize the spaciousness of this contemporary room without detracting from the walls and ceiling.

Install your own acoustical ceilings

Either of two methods of installation may be used for tile or plank ceilings. Both are simple for the home handyman, and they do not require special tools.

If the present ceiling is in relatively good condition, the fastest and most economical method is to cement the tiles or planks to the existing ceiling.

If the ceiling is badly cracked or uneven, or there are exposed joists, such as in basements or attics, the stapling method is best. Start by nailing 1 × 2-inch wood furring strips at right angles to the ceiling joists. Space them on 12-inch centers for 12 × 12-inch tiles, so that all the tile joints will occur over the strips. Then staple the tiles to the strips, keeping them lined up properly. A special tongue-and-groove joint conceals the staples and ensures a level ceiling. It takes planning, but instructions included with the tile will guide you.

Dry-wall panels work well on ceilings and are less expensive than ceiling tile. They are harder to install, however, since you have larger panels to handle. T-braces and a strong friend will come in handy. Cut the panel to size, nail it up, tape the joints, then paint it. Dry wall is ideal for the basement, to conceal exposed joists. By nailing the dry-wall panels to the joists, you can cover a lot of area for very little cost.

Before this kitchen was treated to a complete rejuvenation project, the work area was gloomy and tunnel-like; it resembled a laboratory. In addition to the complete lack of adequate kitchen facilities, decorative features were nonexistent. In planning the remodeling, it was necessary to take both factors into consideration before starting the project.

You can see at right how a dull and uninspiring room has been transformed into one that is functional, decorative, and easy to maintain. The clever ceiling treatment adds sparkle to a room that might otherwise be a little colorless. The bright blue-and-white striped wall covering used to paper the ceiling adds a festive note to the work area. The wide scalloped border visually lowers the ceiling. In the dining area, the blue is repeated in the wall color, and the geometric-design blue and white wall covering used to paper the ceiling. The terracotta coloring of the vinyl floor in a brick design harmonizes with the mellow wood finish of the kitchen cabinets, and window shutters. Yellow café curtains and yellow painted kitchen walls bring sunshine into the room; antique accessories add charm and personality.

Use fabric for overhead drama

Ceiling drama can be the solution if you seek a way to make an ordinary room extraordinary. It is particularly apt where badly placed doors and windows prevent the centering of interest on a wall—the more conventional way to give focus to a decor.

Fabric on the ceiling is not really a new idea. Castles and palaces set styles in such treatments a long time ago. In those days, fabric served as insulation against cold, and also as an acoustical device to prevent sound from echoing against the stone or marble walls of vast, high-ceilinged rooms.

Pictured in accompanying pages are examples of innovative uses of fabrics for ceilings.

For the living room ceiling of a highrise apartment with a spectacular view as a backdrop, a dramatic canopy treatment using filmy, sheer fabric in a floral pattern is completely appropriate. The apple-green and white sheer fabric is applied to the ceiling in shirred panels mounted on rods, with each panel being gathered to meet at the center of the room.

The same fabric has been used for laminated window shades and for tieback curtains. The window shades are mounted on reverse rollers to hide the rollers themselves. And the floor-to-ceiling track runs in front of enclosed radiators and air-conditioning units located just below the windows. Either the draw draperies or the window shades can regulate light and privacy.

The combination of the ceiling and window treatments is a good example of the several different uses to which fabric can be put to add drama to a room. The green in the print is repeated in several large green foliage plants, and in chair cushions; the large gold, curved sofa is a shade darker than the gold of the carpeting and walls, and the red upholstery of the chair in the foreground is repeated in small decorative accessories and flower arrangement.

Styles, as you can see, can be very different, depending upon the fabric, its color, its pattern, and the manner in which it is mounted. Your preference may be for the sophisticated or the romantic; for the tailored or the informal. The effect depends on the fabric you choose, the way you install it, and the decor of the room in which you use it. It can be as correct in an elegant living room as in a dashing bedroom or bath for the very young. And, as you will see on the following pages, the fabric ceiling is also very much the thing for kitchens.

Dining rooms also can benefit from rejuvenation that focuses on overhead drama. Basement recreation rooms whose overhead pipes and beams offer handicaps in remodeling projects can be stylishly reclaimed with the right ceiling installation. (See *Canopies,* p. 696, and *Canvas Panels,* p. 700.)

Paste fabric on the ceiling, or mount it on rods, depending on the kind of fabric you choose and the mood you wish to establish. For sheer fabric to imitate a canopy, a series of curtain rods can be mounted on the wall just below the ceiling. Each panel is shirred down to almost nothing at the center of the ceiling. The effect secured is distinctive and also practical.

A point to remember when using fabric on the ceiling is that cool colors of pale value will make the ceiling seem higher; warm colors and deep hues reduce apparent height.

Carpeting is becoming more popular as a covering for both ceilings and walls. As well as being decorative from the standpoint of color and texture, it has great sound-absorbing properties.

If you would like the effect of a fabric ceiling with even less maintenance, look to the vinyl-coated wallpapers on today's market. Overhead, they'll look like fabric, and the trickery will be even harder to detect if you choose a matching fabric for draperies and slipcovers.

The cheerful ceiling below highlights a child's bedroom. It is wallpaper, with a fabric-like texture, that puts color overhead. Imitating a striped awning effect, an edging of the same striped wall covering borders all four bedroom walls.

If you decide to use a ceiling treatment such as this, measure ceiling accurately, draw a line first from each corner diagonally across the room to the opposite corner. Next draw a line from the center of each wall directly across to the center of the opposite wall. In this way you determine the exact center of the ceiling. This will be the spot from which to start. The striped wallpaper must be measured and cut carefully in order to create this novel and ingenious effect. After the ceiling is completed, the border strips can be cut, then hung so that stripes are a continuation of ceiling stripes for a total matched appearance. The shades of hot reds and pinks with a small amount of contrasting green are lively colors that a young child will like, and are also not confined to the nursery age group.

Small touches of red borrowed from the ceiling wallpaper are used on painted toy chests, chair, picture frames, lamp and other room accessories. Everything else, including the easy-to-clean vinyl floor covering, is kept off-white. Fabrics are long-wearing and washable; the cotton rug is washable, too. In a bedroom of average dimensions such as this one it is important that the neutral tones balance the vivid colors. Otherwise the overuse of brilliant color could result in an oppressive atmosphere.

When you are shopping for wallpaper, remember that it is available in three distinct categories: water-resistant, water sensitive, and plastic. Each type can be cleaned as long as you know just what type of paper you have and how to care for it. Be sure to follow manufacturer's recommendations. To spot-clean fingermarks from untreated papers, simply rub them with art gum. Grease or oil spots can sometimes be removed from wallpaper by pressing a piece of ordinary white blotting paper over the spots with a hot iron. If you choose one of the all-vinyls, they are completely scrubbable. Many wall coverings are pre-pasted, pre-trimmed, and strippable.

Neither are the furnishings in this room confined to an infant. Except for the crib, which can be replaced with a youth-size or full-size bed later on, the rest of the furniture will be suitable during all the growing-up years.

What you can do with wallpaper

Including the ceiling as part of a total wall-covering scheme—papering or covering it in the same fabric as walls—can also be a means of camouflage. In a small room that presents problems because of numerous jogs or other undesirable features in its walls, this handling can be a remarkably imaginative disguise.

Colorful ceiling treatments are worthy of consideration for whatever room you are planning to decorate. The bathroom, for example, lends itself well to dramatic prints or stripes of brilliant color applied to the ceiling. Even if you consider yourself somewhat conservative in taste, you need not worry about going a bit flamboyant here. You do not spend a great deal of time in this room, and bold or dashing patterns and colors that might be oppressive in, say, the living room will be cheerful here.

But although you can be bold in a room where you spend little time, think twice about a dominant ceiling treatment for the living room, especially if you lean toward more conventional decorating styles.

If you are budget-minded, you may choose to achieve a luxury look with an expensive

Paste a flower bed of wallpaper on your ceiling to dramatize a ceiling light fixture. In the photo below, a strip of scenic wallpaper was used over a dining-room table. The brilliant floral colors are echoed in the window blinds, table furnishings, and daisy centerpiece. This is a trick worth copying if you want to spotlight a specific area in one room.

A fanciful ceiling treatment that dominates an attractive decorating scheme sets the pace in the kitchen below. The carved figurehead resembling those that ornamented the bows of Viking ships many years ago is backed up by ash wood curved and shaped to resemble the keel of a ship.

In between the ribs, Thai silk in citron and avocado stripes has been used to cover the ceiling and extends down to the tops of the wall cabinets. The Thai silk wall covering is reemphasized in the dining area beyond. The designs on the cabinet door fronts follow the same curves as the lines of the ceiling ribs above.

wallpaper that dominates the scheme. Often, by concentrating color, design, and pattern in a limited area such as the ceiling only, you can use less of the expensive wallpaper and still gain an effect that brings everything else into focus.

Choose anything from zebra stripes to a giant-size floral pattern in the new wet-look vinyls, sleek foils, or fuzzy flocks for a change. If you want a flocked ceiling with a budget price tag, use a spray gun to spray your own flocked designs on a painted ceiling.

Artist-designed wallpapers intended for center ceiling placement are a clever way to take advantage of the fifth wall. Small rooms—such as bedrooms and hallways—respond as happily to dramatic ceiling decoration as do living rooms. But keep the pattern in scale with the room size.

When selecting wallpaper, choose appropriate styles—those that blend with the pattern you have already established through other furnishings. There are wallpapers to suit every period—from modern to traditional.

How to repair an old ceiling

Check carefully for ceiling damage in an older house. If there are extensive stains visible, do not attempt any ceiling repairs until you have taken care of the real culprit, which may be a leak in an upstairs pipe or in the roof.

Painting is the quick and inexpensive way to refinish ceilings that have no special problems. The preparation method used for walls works just as well here, and you can use the same types of paint, too. If the ceiling is badly cracked, a textured or sand-finish paint is the answer. To patch a ceiling, use one of the new latex patching compounds. Brush a coat of the compound over the cracked area, then embed fiber-glass mesh in it. A second coat covers the mesh, forming a smooth patch that will not break open later. A coat of textured paint will then make a nearly perfect cover-up.

When a small room is shared by two little girls, it takes ingenuity to give it the professional decorating touch. In the room above, a cheerful yellow floral wall covering has been used on the ceiling only; the remainder of the room is done entirely in solid colors of the same tones in the wallpaper pattern. The ceiling is the dominant factor in this decorating scheme, and everything else in the room takes its cue from this colorful print.

Ideas New And Old For Table Decorations

A colorful centerpiece can do much to enhance the beauty of your dining table or buffet and to set a mood—formal or informal—for your meal. Flower and fruit arrangements are the most frequently used types of centerpiece, but there are many other possibilities—candles, small sculptures, potted plants, colorfully iced cakes for special occasions, and decorative objects of every conceivable type.

When you plan a centerpiece, you must first consider the type of meal you will serve. A centerpiece for a sit-down meal has to be fairly low in height, so that it does not interfere with across-the-table conversation. In the past, centerpieces were always designed with a picture in mind of guests seated around a table. Today, however, meals shared with guests are more often than not served buffet style, and in designing the centerpiece for the food-serving area you are free to create a spectacular, soaring arrangement. For example, tall spires of white stock in an ironstone tureen would make a striking decoration for a buffet, but such an arrangement placed between seated diners would force them to lean this way and that in order to converse.

Whether your centerpiece is for a conventional seating arrangement around a dining table or to decorate the buffet or table on which food is placed, you should think first of color. Flowers, foliage, candles, figurines—whatever you use—may match, harmonize, or contrast with colors of linens, china, or glassware. Your centerpiece colors should, however, be part of a considered overall scheme—not a random selection.

Find the right container

Unusual containers can often make the difference between a centerpiece that is pleasant but undistinguished and one that has originality and sparks your entire table setting. Many objects well suited to play this dramatic role may not originally have been containers at all. When looking for such objects, consider your collectibles—things you have saved that are interestingly old, but not old enough to rate as bona fide antiques. Don't mislay them—display them!

If you find you do not have any appropriate collectibles, you might enjoy acquiring some. If you have a special interest in baking, for example, you can look for old-time cooking and baking tools. A fabulous variety of molds, skillets, and pans may be had for small sums at secondhand shops.

Pencil boxes, chalk boxes, and slates that date back to the one-room schoolhouse are another kind of nostalgic curio you could

A bountiful mixed bouquet takes full advantage of the ▶ interesting shape of a white ironstone soup tureen used as a container. The arrangement is basically informal, yet it calls up memories of the past because of its romantically full design and because of the colors used: pale pinks, white, rose, red, and purple. It is a centerpiece of essential femininity and elegance.

On another occasion, the same unconventional container might well hold a mixed bouquet of brilliant summer annuals and be a fitting decoration for a simple supper.

Look again and imagine the tureen filled with boxwood, red carnations, and Christmas greens to decorate a midnight buffet. It all depends on the mood you want to establish for your party.

Keep in mind the added appeal given by an "offbeat" container such as this to centerpieces that will add a fillip to your entertaining regardless of choice of menu.

For an informal fall lunch or supper party, an arrangement of wheat and colorful ears of Indian corn is ideal. Use a wooden salad bowl as a container. Fold a straw place mat of neutral color around the stems of the wheat and secure it with a piece of colored yarn that harmonizes with the corn colors. Place the sheaf of wheat and a bright coleus plant (a croton would be equally effective) at the rear. To make the rosette flowers that are interesting accompaniments, moisten yellowed corn husks, bend the leaves back carefully into rolls that resemble petals, and secure with wire.

Place mats and napkins need not match, but shades of brown, orange, or gold would be particularly suitable for the mood and colors of this centerpiece. For more color on the table, use glasses of deep green or amber.

One-sided arrangements of this sort are effective if your table is to be placed against a wall and guests are to be seated only at one side and at the ends. If guests are to be seated all around the table, adjust your design so that it is equally attractive from all sides. A great time saver when making such an arrangement is to place the container on a lazy Susan; then you can turn it as you work to be sure the design is appealing from every angle.

A graceful arrangement of seasonal fruit and simple flowers, such as marigolds cut from the garden, makes a great standby for last-minute supper parties. Even if you must buy a few flowers, the cost will be minimal, and the effect will be one of easy hospitality your guests will appreciate.

Glass or silver compotes are especially suitable containers for arrangements of this kind. First place the marigolds, inserting the stems into a well-soaked oasis wrapped in dull-green foil—so that it won't show—or into a needlepoint that has its own cup. Next arrange grapes to fall gracefully over the side, carrying your design line downward to tie into the secondary design of mounded fruit and perhaps a few more flowers in a small container.

When the height lines established by the flowers are satisfying and the grapes are placed in a line you like, pile in an assortment of colorful fruit such as red and golden apples, pears, and maybe a banana. Secure the fruit with toothpicks if necessary.

An arrangement that includes no live plant materials at all is a useful thing to have tucked away. Then you can bring it out when you are notified at the last moment that guests are coming to dinner and you have no time to buy or to create a suitable arrangement for your table.

All you need are peacock feathers and some small gourds that have been spray-painted a dull gold. Mount the gourds on an inexpensive tray, gluing them together in an attractive design. In the gaps, insert colorful peacock feathers. If you like, just before your guests arrive, add a few short-stemmed flowers inserted into florist picks that hold a supply of water. Late garden chrysanthemums are particularly attractive with golden gourds and blue-green feathers.

If you live in or near the country, all sorts of pods, cones, pips, and seed heads are yours for the gathering and could be used in the same manner as gourds. For something tall and graceful, pampas grass that can be bought from a florist would make a fine substitute for feathers. Leave the pods and cones in their natural colors or, for variety, gild some of them and leave the rest as is. Protect your arrangement against dust with a plastic cover when not in use.

Some of the simplest centerpieces are the most effective. By trial and error and by studying pictures, you can learn when to stop adding to an arrangement, when to resist the temptation to include an unnecessary figure or ornament in your design, and how not to overdo a good thing.

The centerpiece at left is a good example of the virtue of simplicity. Spray-painted pine cones and tiny green straw flowers accent and emphasize the novel sculptured form. Any further addition would seem to be an afterthought and would detract from the design rather than adding to it.

The Christmas table decoration below is traditionally simple. Gilded magnolia leaves, wired together to resemble flower petals, and a few gold tree ornaments festoon a swag created from long-needled branches of evergreen to form a flowing decoration. Two white pillar candles of different heights complete the arrangement. Understatement and restraint account for a great deal of its charm.

Evergreens will stay fresh for a good many days without water if they are cut just before arranging. To make them last even longer, use needleholders in shallow cups of water. Ivy, holly, pine, and mistletoe are traditional favorites. When you use them on your Christmas table, you will be honoring age-old symbols of good cheer shared with others.

collect and use as accompaniments to imaginative centerpieces. You can find collectibles almost anywhere—the older they are, the better, and the more interesting as decor for your most festive table settings.

How to use fruits and vegetables
Nonfloral materials that are decorative, unusual, and eye-catching make excellent centerpieces. Vegetables, for example, are just as attractive as flowers to accompany an informal meal. You might make a cornucopia of cleanly scrubbed garden vegetables, using parsley sprigs for greenery. Almost any vegetables can be used to decorate a table. A "wreath" of pine studded with artichokes and mushrooms makes an unusual and attractive centerpiece, as does a mound of eggplants and onions. Even everyday vegetables such as potatoes and carrots can be used in imaginative ways.

One giant bloom—such as the spectacular dahlia at left—is perfect for a summer dinner party. The Renaissance-type compote is just the right size for displaying the blossom, yet it is not so tall that diners must crane their necks to carry on cross-table conversation. A similar effect could be achieved with bunched smaller flowers—marigolds, zinnias, asters, chrysanthemums, or any others with rounded blooms of many petals. The collar of foliage lends the centerpiece the appealing look of an old-fashioned bouquet.

Reflect summer's carefree mood with informal designs for a ▶ centerpiece to grace a supper on the porch. Use whatever is most plentiful in your July and August garden, and include lots of cooling green foliage with hot flower colors. Choose the more durable flowers and foliage for hot-weather arrangements. Nothing is less appealing on a warm day than the sight of drooping flowers.

The free-flowing arrangement at right, in shades of pink, magenta, and purple, was inspired by the frosty blue of the glass tabletop. Clipped from a summer border, the flowers include zinnias, phlox, rosy loosestrife for height, and trailing stems of petunias for a graceful line.

On the table below, short-stemmed camellias and green foliage were arranged in two shallow, rectangular containers, separated at the center by a cooling piece of glass sculpture. Fully opened roses or tuberous begonias would also be effective in this sort of arrangement. If you would like to use centerpieces like this often, have a metalsmith make containers to suit the dimensions of your table.

Fruits, too, are lovely to look at—and they can become the dessert once the main course has been eaten. A compote filled with fruit and garnished with a few green leaves is a classic centerpiece. If you want to do something a little different, try making a "strawberry tree" by impaling plump berries on toothpicks inserted into plastic foam.

Summery centerpieces

Summer centerpieces should take full advantage of the charm of informality. A relaxed living pattern, with meals often served on porch or patio, has a special appeal in the warmer months. The fact that dinner is served in an informal setting is no reason to forgo the pleasure of flowers on the table.

How to arrange a centerpiece

Arranging is easy, once you learn a few fundamentals. Basic to the success of an arrangement is good equipment. The essentials are relatively few and quite inexpensive.

All you need for floral arrangements—other than flowers—are: three or four containers in basic shapes (low, tall, round, and rectangular); an assortment of needlepoint holders; and other stem-securing equipment such as crushed chicken wire, a knife, or shears, florist's tape, and clay.

Shape, size, and color of containers are of first importance. Until you become a collector of bowls and vases, shun those that are bright colored or patterned.

Neutral shades of off-white, green, gray, beige, and brown will not compete with flower hues. For the infrequent occasions when a vivid container is needed, see if you can make use of things you have in the house. An ash tray, a casserole, or a coffee mug may have hitherto unrecognized potentials as a colorful, original container.

You can often find inspiration for an unusual centerpiece for your table or buffet on a calendar. Most holidays have traditional associations of colors, motifs, and meanings easy to use as the basis for striking table decorations.

The handsome table above would be inviting at any time of year, but the arrangement of bright red apples, blue candles, and greenery under the outspread wings of a gilded American eagle would be especially suitable for an informal supper on a day with patriotic associations.

Major holidays suggest obvious decorations, but creating arrangements for more obscure celebrations can be great fun, too. A miniature maypole for May Day or a mound of vegetables with toy tractors and trucks on Labor Day are only two ideas that you might try for unusual centerpieces.

A bowl or compote of fresh fruit on a table serves a dual purpose, at once charmingly decorative and deliciously functional. At meal's end guests can eat the table decoration for dessert. For sheer elegance a silver or porcelain epergne filled with fruit, such as the one at right, is unmatched. Grapes or strawberries are always a good choice.

Fundamentals of arrangement

Conditioning flowers before you arrange them is very important if you expect your centerpiece to last. If you are cutting from your own garden, do so early in the morning or late in the afternoon. Flowers tend to wilt much more rapidly when cut in the middle of a hot summer day.

Use a sharp knife and cut stems on a diagonal to gain maximum surface for water intake. Plunge stems into lukewarm water at once. Carry the flowers indoors to as cool a place as possible and leave them in water almost up to their heads for 4 to 5 hours or overnight before making your arrangement.

For woody stems (roses, lilacs, etc.) ensure lavish intake of water by paring off bark two inches from the bottom and cross-cut or pound the peeled section with a hammer before plunging the stems into water. After conditioning, cut the stems again before arranging.

On the beautiful table above hardly anything could be more appropriate than a silver tray heaped with green and golden pears and flanked by crystal swans. Take particular notice of the simplicity of this table decoration. No superfluous leaf, blossom, or accessory obscures the inviting dazzle created by the sheens and textures of silver, fruit, crystal, glassware, and polished wood. Note, too, that the colors of the pears echo and emphasize the room's color scheme.

Vegetables can be beautiful—or charming or handsome or delicate or whatever—depending on how they are displayed, and they are quite suitable on a festive table set for an informal luncheon or supper party. They are not appropriate on a table, however, if the occasion is at all formal.

In the centerpiece at right, the rich wood tones of a highly polished burl base make a good contrast to the paler autumnal colors of fruit and vegetables. A sprouted onion and scrubbed carrots are amusing additions to an arrangement of peppers, grapes, and squash. A pine branch secured in a needlepoint holder hidden under the vegetables gives height and added interest to this one-sided composition.

How To Create A Focal Point And Use It As A Keynote For Furnishings

Every serious artist knows that there must be one central point of interest in a picture to which all other elements are harmoniously subservient. Failure to state a focal point clearly—or inclusion of several competing "centers"—will produce an ineffective painting, one in which the eye will wander all over the surface seeking in vain for the focus.

In decorating a room, much the same principle applies. Without one particular element that is obviously dominant, the room fails to "hang together" and projects a restless mood. It gives the observer a feeling that selection of furnishings was largely the result of chance, not a thoughtful matter of design and intent.

One of the first criteria for deciding upon a center of interest in room decoration is that it be large enough to catch attention immediately. Its size must, of course, be related to the size of the room. In a very small room—an entry, for example—the focal point might be an object as small as a coat tree, if it is sufficiently interesting in design. But in a large living room, the focal point will have to be in scale with the room size—large enough to be noticed as soon as one enters. The fireplace wall, opposite, is a good example of a center of interest important enough to dominate the decoration of a large room.

Walls are, in fact, most often used as centers of interest in decorating, just because they are large enough to capture attention. Mural wall coverings, groupings of paintings, or collections of china, glass, or similar objects offer excellent possibilities as centers of interest. Less often used in this way but also a good choice is the decorated ceiling.

Floors, too, can be made focal points in decorating. Handsome area rugs or Oriental rugs—originals or good copies—can establish colors, style, and mood for an entire decorating scheme.

Next in importance to scale in establishing a valid center of interest is the way furniture is grouped. Placing tables, sofas, and chairs so that they lead the eye to the focal point can make the difference between success and failure. Examine the arrangements of furniture in the pages that follow for ideas you can use in your home to emphasize a center of interest.

Give star status to one feature of your decorating scheme; let it be the unifying element in the total design of a room, and your success is almost guaranteed.

One of the most effective ways to establish that all-important center of interest is to focus attention on one wall of the room. It may be largely done for you by architectural design (as in the case of the fireplace wall opposite). In this case, take care not to detract from it by a furniture arrangement that blocks the view or by introducing too many competing accents and accessories.

In this room, an architectural feature—a fireplace wall that ▶ includes clerestory windows and a raised hearth—is the obvious center of interest. The texture and color of stones used in fireplace construction are as interesting to the eye as a painting. Wisely, other elements are played down so that the fireplace wall holds attention.

Natural wood colors, neutral carpet color, off-white ceiling, and subdued color and pattern of sofa upholstery all contribute to playing up the roughhewn attraction of interior stone.

The scene visible through the clerestory windows above the fireplace is as spectacular as any painting, and it has been properly emphasized both by the architectural design and by the simplicity of furnishings.

Given a dramatic setting by wood paneling installed like a picture frame, a colorful wall plaque against an off-white background forms a striking focal point for this room.

The dimensions of the niche were planned to fit exactly the sofa placed below the plaque; its covering of Siamese silk advances the Oriental theme, as does the gilded statue placed in the corner and surrounded by foliage plants that disguise the pedestal on which it stands.

In a room that lacks an architectural feature to dictate the nature and placement of a center of interest, a device of this sort can be very effective—but only if it is truly allowed to dominate. It is dominant here against the neutral wood-paneled walls, the adroitly placed furniture, the subdued colors of upholstery fabric, and the restrained accents.

Against a painted wall, a panel of mural wallpaper might be handled in a manner similar to this with good results.

More often, you will have to establish the center of interest yourself, by means of dramatic wall decorations, a combination of wall and window treatments, or, as you will see on a following page, with an assemblage of paintings or *objets d'art*.

Once you have decided upon the element in your total decor that is to serve as the center of interest, think carefully before you add items that could deflect attention from the primary motif.

Accent and accessory pieces should always relate (in color, style, or mood) to your center of interest, making it clear that they are satellites, not competitors for the eye of the beholder. A good example of competent handling of this problem is presented in the room pictured opposite. The scale, placement, and color of the wall decoration catch your attention first; then, adding to the appeal, you notice the Oriental sculpture in the corner at right. Its presence reinforces the Oriental theme, but you do not mistake the statue for the major item of decorative interest.

A good rule to follow if in doubt about the addition of accent pieces, once you've established a center of interest: *Do not.*

Wall arrangements

Picture groupings can be one of the most elegant of centers of interest—if handled with taste, and if the individual items in the collection are worthy of attention. If you are a collector of prints, lithographs, etchings, drawings, or paintings, this will be a satisfying way both to establish the focal point of a room's decor and to display a group of your favorites.

In a den or family room, the work of the photographic hobbyist can be shown to good effect, but photographs do not lend themselves well to the very formal setting.

Kitchens are hospitable to similar groupings of flower and herb prints, favorite recipes, children's bright paintings. (See *Accents and Accessories,* Vol. 1.)

French doors revealing an unattractive view were the dominant feature of this high-ceilinged room. It took imagination to turn a handicap into an asset, a center of interest. Using translucent shades laminated in black and white striped duck from floor to ceiling, the doors were hidden and the effect of the high ceiling was emphasized.

By framing the shades with antique white satin tie-back draperies and hanging an important picture between the windows, a striking wall was established as the room's center of interest.

A fireplace of mellow brick is dramatically centered in an angular window that looks out on woods. Part of an addition to the original living room, it has been made a center of interest for the enlarged room.

Flagstone used for the fireplace border and the foot-high raised hearth acts as a window ledge. Fixed windows at the ceiling level are framed in cedar to match beams.

Accent light fixtures in the ceiling focus on the fireplace, maintaining it as the center of interest after sundown.

Walls put to work as focal points in a room's decoration offer infinite possibilities. They can go formal to suit that style of furnishings, or they can be homespun and rustic if that is the prevailing mood.

In a room that has a fireplace, that wall is almost certain to be your choice when you seek to establish a center of interest. Whether a fire is burning or not, there is a magnetic appeal about a hearth that just naturally attracts attention.

If it is at all possible to use the structural features of your home as centers of interest, do. A picture window is an excellent focal point anywhere in the house, providing a constantly changing view of the world outside. A stairway can be an asset if the room is planned around it.

A striped canopy in hot citrus colors cheerfully dominates the ▶ decor of a sun porch designed for day-into-evening entertaining. For a neat, taut look, the canopy is stretched and attached to a wooden frame at each end. Paint and fabric pick up the canvas colors for walls and other furnishings, and shiny black upholstery on several pieces creates welcome contrast.

This type of treatment is especially well suited to remodelings of basements and attics, where odd wall angles sometimes present decorating problems. Inexpensive and simple enough for an average handyman or woman to execute, it is a way to achieve a center of interest that should be of special appeal to those who are decorating on a budget.

An eclectic wall arrangement is the center of interest in the kitchen below. Appropriately for the kitchen, all the pictures are prints of fruits and vegetables; some follow a traditional style, others are contemporary. By mounting the pictures on pegboard, you can shift them and regroup them to suit your mood or the occasion. And the pegboard coordinates the counter tops and the yellow floral arrangement. For variety, the wall grouping could include cross-stitch samplers, crewel work pictures, and children's art.

In dramatic contrast to the bright yellow tone is the handsome black and gold refrigerator and black lacquered cabinets trimmed with gold molding and hardware. The intensity of the hue serves to highlight the picture grouping by providing a sharp contrast between the pegboard and the floor.

A center of interest should catch the attention, hold it, and draw the spectator deeper into the room. Mirrors are arresting focal points because they do just this, giving back an eye-catching image of the room. Unusual functional objects, such as a round table with a sunken center holding plants or fish, provide a fascinating centerpiece for a room. A piano usually attracts so much attention that it might as well be included when planning a room's focal center. Almost as magnetic as a wall fireplace are today's freestanding stoves and working replicas of antique models.

In a room that lacks a natural focus such as a fireplace or a large view window, you can create a center of interest that will capture everyone's attention. Hang one magnificent picture on a wall and place furniture below and beside it to emphasize its importance. Lamps, as they are used in the room above left, or ceiling spots will maintain its dominance when the sun goes down.

Scenes similar to this can be purchased as a section of mural wall covering, cut out, matted if you like, and framed to suit the style of other furnishings, with the colors of both the mural and the frame used in chairs and tables.

In a less formal room, a greatly enlarged photograph—of a mountain, woods, or stream—could be used similarly. These, too, are available commercially if there is no camera hobbyist in your family.

A fire pit in the middle of the room rather than in a wall becomes the focal point of interest in the comfortable family room pictured here at left. Constructed of fieldstone that was gathered on the owners' land, it is rustic in style. Suited to its mood are the paneled walls made of weathered barn siding—a finishing material so popular that it is becoming difficult to find. Floors are of practical, hard-surface vinyl—easy to wipe clean after a barbecue session.

The suspended metal hood above the fire pit was painted a charcoal color, as was the ceiling, helping to focus attention on the cheeriness of the open fire pit, which is adjacent to the kitchen in this remodeled cottage.

Architectural design made it nearly inevitable that this fire-▶ place wall should be the center of interest in the room at right. To guarantee that it will be, it has been painted with flat black paint, except for a light border around the opening of the fireplace proper. Using fireplace colors for the window treatment, neutral shades for most furnishings, and touches of red to add spice restates the importance of the fireplace.

Notice that furniture shapes, too, continue the clean and uncluttered lines of the fireplace. A modern accent rug in front of the hearth brings a small amount of pattern into the scene, but limits colors to black, white, brown, and gold that harmonize with the solid-color vinyl flooring.

Master/Guide

Bookcases and Bookshelves

Bookcases and bookshelves not only fulfill their traditional function but provide solutions to a number of decorative problems as well. Adaptable to any style theme and suitable for any room in your home, they offer almost unlimited decorative possibilities. See *Bookcases and Bookshelves,* Vol. 3, p. 546, continued on p. 579; see also *Accessories and Accents,* Vol. 1; *Budget Ideas,* p. 598; and *Dividers,* Vol. 7.

Borders

Edgings of patterns or contrasting colors can brighten and define a decorating scheme of predominantly solid colors. Available in many styles, borders of paper, fabric, and modern synthetics are easy to apply and have a multitude of decorative uses. See *Borders,* p. 584; see also *Trimmings,* Vol. 17.

Boss

Chiefly an architectural term, referring to a raised ornament placed at intersections of moldings or beams. Bosses have also been used on furniture, particularly in the seventeenth and eighteenth centuries. Usually oval

or round in form, the boss was inspired by Gothic decorations, such as those found on the vaulted ceilings of many European cathedrals. The most frequently employed motifs are flowers, foliage, and heads of angels.

Boston rocker with stenciled back rail.

Boston Rocker

A rocking chair with a seat that curves upward at the rear and downward in front. Of nineteenth-century American design, the chair has a spindle back. There is usually a flower decoration stenciled in gilt on the wide top rail of the back, and sometimes this motif is found on the seat as well.

Bottle-end Glazing

A bull's-eye pattern or a design of circular bottom-of-the-bottle glass discs leaded together. This type of decoration was used on cabinet doors in the sixteenth, seventeenth, and eighteenth centuries.

Bouclé

French word meaning buckled or curly, applied to textiles made with yarn that is looped irregularly on the surface to create a rough finish. Bouclé yarns are often used for modern upholstery fabrics.

Boudoir

Term derived from the French verb *bouder,* meaning to pout, and used to refer to a lady's dressing room, bedroom, or sitting room. A well-appointed boudoir was indispensable to the fashionable lady in court circles of seventeenth- and eighteenth-century France. There she was at her most feminine. Her boudoir was a retreat where she could read, weep, make plans, write letters, and receive guests.

Boulle, André Charles (1642-1732)

French cabinetmaker to Louis XIV, who designed and executed the famous mirror walls, as well as paneling, wood floors, and other decorations, for the palace at Versailles. Boulle was and is best known for an ornate style of marquetry he invented and used on chests and cabinets. He devised a technique of gluing together sheets of metal (usually brass) and tortoiseshell, cutting designs from the double sheets, and then using the cut-out pieces as inlays (metal into tortoiseshell or vice versa). His name—sometimes spelled Boull or Buhl—has become synonymous with pieces decorated in this elaborate manner.

Bourbon Style

Term applied to furniture produced during the Bourbon monarchy (1824-1830) in France and essentially a continuation of styles that had their inception during the late Empire.

Bow Back

The curved or hooplike back of the classical Windsor chair, which was introduced in the eighteenth century. The lines of the curve continue down to the arms or the seat.

Bow Front

The outward curving front of a chest or similar piece of furniture, also called a swell front. Many bowfront chests and sideboards were produced during the latter half of the eighteenth century. The style was often used by the leading furniture designers of the period, such as Adam and Hepplewhite, and bowfront pieces were particularly popular in England.

Armoire made by André Charles Boulle.

Bow Porcelain

Soft-paste porcelain produced in the eighteenth century at Stratford-le-Bow, a district in the East End of London. The factory at Bow probably began making porcelain in the mid-1740's, but it produced nothing of remarkable quality during its early years of operation. In 1750 a new factory was established, and during the next ten years Bow became one of the largest English porcelain centers of its time.

Bow porcelain covered dish.

Using a soft paste to which bone ash was added, the Bow manufactory produced white tablewares decorated with Oriental designs in underglaze blue, vases decorated with Rococo masks and foliage, and figurines in imitation of Meissen models. All Bow porcelain is characterized by a rather unsophisticated style; modeling tends toward simplicity rather than subtlety, and painting is often poor. Nevertheless, many pieces of merit were produced.

Bow Top

Term describing the top rail of a chair formed as an unbroken curve between the uprights.

Bow Window

A curved bay window. Often large, sometimes semicircular, bow windows are usually located at structural corners.

Box Bed

One that is enclosed on three of its four sides, or occasionally, one that can be folded up against a wall. The type of the more common definition is designed to offer protection against the cold.

Box Pleat

A type of fabric pleating in which the material is folded back on itself, then folded back again in the opposite direction, so that one panel remains hidden. Box pleating is often used for a finish border on slipcovered or upholstered chairs and sofas.

Box Settle

A boxlike piece of furniture that has a hinged lid and a high, straight back and serves both as a chest and a seat. The design was developed during the Renaissance in England and later became a popular feature of the Early American style.

Box Spring

An item of bedding placed beneath the mattress to increase resiliency. Of fairly recent origin, it consists of steel springs enclosed in a boxlike frame. The springs are covered with cotton felt, hair, or a layer of foam rubber, and the entire unit is encased in ticking.

Boxwood

Wood obtained from shrubs of the genus *Buxus* and characterized by a delicate yellow color and close, uniform graining. Boxwood is used primarily for inlaying darker woods.

Boys' Rooms

Rooms for growing boys should ideally be playrooms, studyrooms, and workrooms as well as bedrooms. With contemporary furnishings and some good ideas for multipurpose decorating you can create an attractive, easy-to-care-for room for your youngster that will please his tastes and suit his needs. See *Boys' Rooms,* p. 586; see also *Children's Rooms,* Vol. 5.

Bracket

In furniture, a triangular support piece between the legs and seat of a chair, or between the top and legs of a table. The term is also used to describe wall-hung decorative pieces, such as sconces and small display shelves.

Bracket Foot

A furniture foot in a bracket shape with a curved inner edge and a straight or curved corner. Used chiefly on chests of drawers, desks, and bookcases, the design was popular in eighteenth-century styles in England and America. The three-drawer bureau in the room pictured here has bracket feet.

Braided Rugs

Originally, handmade floor coverings created from scraps of woolens and other fabrics in various colors. The fabrics were cut into long strips, the edges were sewn under, and the strips were braided together and shaped into rugs of round or oval form. Today, braided rugs are usually factory produced.

Brand Names

Unknown brands of merchandise are frequently cheaper than well-known brands. In the long run, however, a lower purchase price on a major item can cost you money. "You get what you pay for" still holds true, and brand names backed up by service guarantees are still the best guide to quality. See *Brand Names,* p. 595.

Early American furnishings, including a bracket-footed chest and a colorful braided rug.

Brass

A metal alloy composed principally of copper and zinc, in varying proportions. The word *brasses* usually refers to decorative items such as handles, hinges, and pulls used on furniture made of wood. It is also used to describe escutcheons or memorial plaques made of this metal alloy.

Brazier

Principally, a metal pan supported on legs, in which hot embers are placed for heating purposes. The term is also applied to an artisan who works in brass.

Bread Box

In Early American antiques, a metal (usually tin) box for bread storage. A characteristic feature is holes punched to form designs, both for decorative purposes and to ventilate the bread. Today bread boxes are made of metal or plastic, and decorations are usually applied to the surface rather than punched in.

Breakfast Rooms

A special room or area designed for convenient serving and minimum care can establish a cheerful atmosphere to start your family off on a pleasant day. After the morning rush is over, a breakfast room is an ideal place for light meals, a coffee klatch with the neighbors, or after-school snacks. See *Breakfast Rooms,* p. 596; see also *Dining Areas,* Vol. 7.

Eighteenth-century English breakfront.

Breakfront

A casemade piece of furniture, characterized by a front constructed on two or more planes, usually with a central projecting section. Specifically, the term has come to be used to describe bookcases and cabinets typical of eighteenth-century furniture design in England and America. The upper section has leaded glass doors, and enclosed shelves and drawers form the lower half. The breakfront illustrated here is decorated with intarsia.

Breaking Strength

In textiles, a term applied to fibers that refers to the amount of weight that can be supported by a single strand.

Breezeway

A covered and sometimes partly enclosed space that connects a house and an adjacent garage. Often screened, breezeways are most frequently found in houses of modern design built in areas with mild climates. Because it is a simple way of creating an outdoor living room, the breezeway is becoming a popular feature in remodeling projects.

Breuer, Marcel Lajos (born 1902)

Modern architect and furniture designer. Born in Hungary, Breuer was associated with the Bauhaus in Weimar and later in Dessau, Germany, where he became a disciple of the idea of functional design. He came to the United States in 1937 and subsequently taught design at Harvard University for a few years before embarking on a long and productive architectural career.

Breuer is responsible for much impressive architecture in both American and European cities, but he is perhaps most widely known as the inventor of the tubular steel chair, one of the most important innovations in furniture design of the twentieth century. Designed in 1925, the Breuer chair features cantilevered tubing to provide firm, comfortable support.

Brewster Chair

A wooden armchair owned by William Brewster (1560-1644), who came to America on the Mayflower and was one of the leaders of Plymouth Colony. It has rows of turned spindles on the back, on the arms, and in the space between the bottom of the arms and the floor. Massive and somewhat crude, in basic design it has the lines of Jacobean furniture and some blending of Tudor and Renaissance elements. Chairs made in imitation of the original, now in Pilgrim Hall, Plymouth, are known as Brewster chairs.

Bric-a-brac

A miscellaneous collection of small objects chosen for their sentimental or antiquarian interest and often displayed in cabinets or on wall shelves. In decorating, the term is especially associated with the Victorian style of displaying a collection of curios.

Bridal Chest

A term used interchangeably with *hope chest* or *dower chest* to describe a piece of furniture in which an unmarried girl stores linens and other household furnishings as she accumulates them. Usually boxlike in shape, it is often cedar-lined and decorated with painted or carved designs. The great majority of bridal chests are in traditional styles, and the custom of keeping them has lost much of its popularity in the modern era.

Bristol Ceramics

Pottery and porcelain made in Bristol, England. A pottery center since the Middle Ages, Bristol produced much notable ceramic work in the eighteenth century. Manufactories there made tin-glazed earthenware, commonly known as delftware, as well as wares in both soft-paste and hard-paste porcelain. Typical earthenware products were plates, teapots, and mugs; soft-paste porcelain was used chiefly in the manufacture of sauceboats; and

Bristol porcelain figurine.

hard-paste porcelain was used for table services, teapots, vases, and figures. Some Bristol hard-paste porcelain pieces were highly elaborate, decorated with flowers and foliage, usually in leaf-green or deep red.

Bristol Glass

Glassware made in Bristol, England, from the seventeenth century onward. About 1745, when the Glass Excise Act was passed, the production of decorated and colored glass became an important industry in England. In subsequent years the numerous factories in Bristol produced some of the most beautiful glassware ever made. Vases, candlesticks, decanters, and flasks, often deep blue, purple, or green, were produced in quantity. Bristol blue glass is considered especially fine, as is Bristol milk glass, which is very thin and has a distinctive creamy color.

British Colonial

Variations on furniture and architectural styles of the West Indies, India, and other colonies of the British Empire.

Broadcloth

Originally, a cotton fabric of tight, unpatterned weave, with a crosswise rib or, sometimes, a twill rib. In earlier centuries this material was used primarily in the making of draperies and bed curtains. Today the term *broadcloth* refers to textiles made of wool and mixed fibers as well as cotton. These fabrics are used for items of clothing and for household furnishings such as draperies, curtains, slipcovers, and linings.

Broadloom

Modern carpeting, in widths of 6, 9, 12, 15, or more feet, of a seamless construction. Broadloom carpeting made of wool, man-made fibers, or mixtures is available in a wide range of textures, weaves, and colors. Although broadloom can be cut from a roll and bound in room size, the term is most commonly associated with wall-to-wall carpeting. Seamless carpeting like the soft green broadloom in the room pictured here is the standard floor covering in most American homes.

Contemporary furnishings, including a broadloom carpet.

Brocade

A fabric, usually silk, that has raised patterns resembling embroidery. In weaving, some weft threads are carried in loose groups on the back surface of the fabric, usually satin or a similar weave, giving that side the effect of embroidery. In the past, clothing of rich and sumptuous brocades, often made with gold or silver threads, was popular among the royalty and nobility of many wealthy courts in Europe and Asia. Today's brocades are used most often as upholstery and drapery in rooms decorated in period styles.

Brocatelle

A heavy fabric similar to brocade, with a raised pattern on the surface, but less finely woven. Brocatelle originated in imitation of Italian tooled leather as weavers sought to duplicate the effect of an embossed pattern on fabric. Traditionally, the pattern is large and is created with a satin weave against a twill background.

Manufacture of both brocades and brocatelles was common in most European countries as early as the twelfth and thirteenth centuries. The development of the jacquard loom in the early nineteenth century made it possible to produce these fabrics in quantity, and they remain popular today, although the distinction between the two is seldom made. Unsuitable for clothing, brocatelle has always been used for drapery and upholstery.

The term *brocatelle* is also used to refer to a kind of marble quarried in Italy, Spain, and France whose surface patterns and grainings resemble brocade.

Sixteenth-century picture frame topped by a broken arch.

Broken Arch

In furniture design, the top of a curved arch whose scrolls or side lines do not meet at the center. The open section is usually filled with a decorative device such as an urn.

Broken Pediment

In furniture design, a decorative element in the shape of a pediment with an opening in the center of the top. The broken pediment was often used in eighteenth-century English styles as a top for bookcases, cabinets, and chests. Part of the space is usually filled with a decorative motif such as a vase.

Broken Stripe Veneer

A thin layer of wood affixed to the surface of a piece of furniture for decorative purposes. The veneer pattern is a stripe broken at irregular intervals by interwoven twisted or spiral grain produced by quarter cutting.

Bronze

A metal alloy, chiefly of copper and tin, sometimes with the addition of small quantities of other elements. Ever since the Bronze Age began—about 3500 B.C. in Europe and probably earlier in Africa and Asia—bronze has been used by craftsmen and artists for weapons, household articles, and statuary.

Brussels Carpet

Carpeting named for the city of Brussels, Belgium, where it was originated. Woven with a three- or four-ply worsted yarn, it has uncut loops drawn up to appear on the surface and form a pattern. The backing is usually of cotton. Because of its deep, uncut pile, Brussels carpet is noted for its long wear.

This type of carpeting was introduced at the important English carpet manufacturing town of Wilton in the mid-eighteenth century. Today *Wilton carpet* refers to the original Brussels type and also to carpets with uncut pile or a combination of cut and uncut pile.

Buckeye

A colloquial term for a work of art, especially a painting, that has been produced with quick sale in view and has no real artistic merit. Works described as buckeyes are usually romantic or sentimental in style.

Buckram

A stiff cotton fabric of plain weave used primarily as an interlining in valances and drapery headings to provide reinforcement. Originally, the name was applied to a richly woven, heavy fabric of fine linen or cotton that was valued as a material for clothing.

Budget Ideas

Good decorating need not be expensive. There are hundreds of practical and attractive ways to decorate your home without spending a small fortune in the process. See *Budget Ideas,* p. 598.

Buffets

Built in or freestanding, buffets are invaluable for informal entertaining. They provide not only the tabletop space you need to spread everything out but also storage space. See *Buffets,* p. 650; see also *Dining Areas,* Vol. 7.

Built-in Lighting

Yesterday's lighting fixtures hung from the ceiling or projected from the wall, and they frequently were important items in a decorative style. Today's lighting devices are often concealed. Thoughtfully planned, lighting can enhance a room as well as illuminate it and can set any mood you want. See *Built-in Lighting,* p. 656; see also *Lighting,* Vol. 11.

Built-ins

In the modern home there is no such thing as too much storage space. Built-ins are not too difficult for the average handyman to make, and it is surprisingly easy to design a unit that will exactly suit both your room style and your storage needs. See *Built-ins,* p. 666; see also *Storage,* Vol. 15.

Bull's-eye

Term applied to the typical distortion in the center of a round window or mirror made of curved glass. Bull's-eye windows, with either concave or convex glass, are used in areas where it is desirable to transmit light but to obscure the view. Bull's-eye mirrors are convex and are found chiefly in American furnishings.

Bunks

Throughout history, bunks have provided an answer to the problem of many people and little sleeping space. If you have children, the chances are that you face the same problem. Consider the bunk; it is one traditional space saver that has not been outmoded. See *Bunks,* p. 670; see also *Boys' Rooms,* p. 586, and *Children's Rooms,* Vol. 5.

Bureau

The French term for a desk or writing table, derived from the word *bure,* the coarse cloth with which such pieces were originally covered. In England the word also refers to a desk, but in the United States it usually describes a bedroom chest of drawers.

Burgundian Style

Furniture style developed in the late sixteenth century in the French region of Burgundy. Massive in construction, Burgundian furniture has many typical Renaissance elements, including the use of architectural elements and carved decorations of human or mythological figures. The originator of the style was Hughes Sambin, an architect who worked in Dijon.

Burl

A grain pattern found at the center of a section of wood cut horizontally from the bottom portion of a tree trunk. The characteristic pattern is the product of cutting across many small, partially formed buds and the pithy center section of the tree. Burl wood is used as thin, decorative veneering on various pieces of casebuilt furniture.

Burlap

Coarsely woven fabric made of jute, hemp, or sometimes cotton, which is used in furniture construction as webbing or as a covering for springs. Burlap was once best known as the material of the bags in which potatoes and other heavy produce were transported to market. Today, in a slightly more refined weave and perhaps dyed, the fabric is popular as wall covering, draperies, and bedspreads. It is usually combined with informal or very modern furnishings.

Butt Joint

In furniture construction, the simplest and least expensive way to join two pieces of wood at a corner. One piece is set against the other and the two are joined with nails or screws, sometimes reinforced by an application of glue. Butt joints are not strong enough to use in places where the wood will be under strain.

Butterfly Table

A drop-leaf table that takes its name from a butterfly-shaped bracket used to support the

leaf when raised. This design, illustrated in the sketch, was originated during the American colonial period.

Buttonwood

Wood of the North American plane tree, often used in furniture construction. The tree bears small hanging fruit and is also called the buttonball tree.

Buttonwood veneers are cut from the section of the tree near its roots, where graining, in a cross section, has an attractive crinkled texture. This texture is produced by the growth pattern of the tree when roots branch off irregularly. Buttonwood veneers are also known as stump grains.

Cabanas

The lucky few who live at water's edge and the many more who own swimming pools should think of building a cabana. Basically simple, functional structures, cabanas can be as luxurious as you want to make them. For convenience, charm, and comfort on the beach, near a lake, or at poolside, they can not be surpassed. See *Cabanas,* p. 674.

Cabinets

The French word *cabinet* has several meanings: a closet or a study or a collection. The English word also has multiple meanings, but to the American homemaker *cabinet* means a place to put things away. Any casebuilt piece with shelves and/or drawers—whether attached to a wall, built-in, or freestanding—is generally called a cabinet, and every home needs some. In selecting or building your cabinets, there are many construction tips you should know about woods, corners, drawers, doors, and shelves. See *Cabinets,* p. 676; *Bathrooms,* Vol. 3; and *Kitchens,* Vols. 10, 11.

Cabriole Chair

A small chair designed by the English furniture maker Thomas Chippendale (1718?-1779), which has a stuffed back and an upholstered seat.

Cabriole Leg

An S-shaped furniture leg. Evolved from heavy baroque turnings and scrolls, the graceful cabriole leg was widely used on chairs and casebuilt furniture in France and England during the eighteenth century. It is a feature of both Louis XV and Queen Anne styles of furniture. Early forms of cabriole leg resemble the bent leg of a capering animal and give the clue to the meaning of the name: *caper* de-

Wing chair with modified cabriole legs.

rives from the Latin word for goat. In time the bends at the "shoulder" and the "knee" of the leg were softened, producing a double curve of elegant sinuosity. From France and England the popularity of the cabriole line spread to Flanders and Italy, and artisans in those countries used it in many designs.

Cabriolet

A small Louis XV armchair with a concave back and cabriole legs. A characteristic decoration of this chair was a bow motif at the center top of its back, suggesting that it was to be hung on a wall.

Cachepot

A decorative container of china, pottery, wood, or metal designed to hold a common flower pot. The term derives from French and translates literally as pot hider.

Eighteenth-century cachepot of St. Cloud porcelain.

Café Curtains

Curtains made in two sections, one short and resembling a valance, to be hung at the top of the window; the other longer, hung from the middle of the window and usually reaching the sill. This type of curtain was created to give some privacy to patrons seated next to the windows of French cafés, yet still admit light through the upper half of the window. Café curtains are now used most frequently with provincial decors, and in kitchens and bathrooms.

Calendering

A final-stage process used in textile manufacturing that consists of running fabric between two hollow, heated cylinders to give a finished, smooth, or shiny surface. The process is used especially in the manufacture of chintzes, polished cottons, and other fabrics with glazed surfaces. It is also employed to smooth uneven or slightly bumpy portions of cloth. The calendering process is also used, for similar purposes, in paper manufacture.

Calico

Originally, a cotton material imported from the Indian city of Calicut, a major port for commerce with Europe during the sixteenth century.

The name calico has, at various times, been applied to many different kinds of cotton fabric. In present-day usage, it refers to a material of a plain, close weave, with a printed pattern on one side. Patterns are usually small, all-over prints of flowers or figures, in colors suitable for use with furnishings of provincial character—American, French, or Italian. Not heavy enough to withstand a great deal of wear, calico is rarely used as an upholstery material, but it is a popular choice for slipcovers, draperies, and bedspreads. In weight and quality, it is similar to the cotton fabric known as percale.

Calligraphy

The art of beautiful writing. The chief aim of calligraphy is to please the eye, and at times this has been accomplished at the expense of clarity. The best calligraphy, however, combines beauty and legibility.

Four examples of Western calligraphy.

cult to read. At the beginning of the Renaissance the Gothic script was considered inappropriate for the rendering of the classics, and the Roman printed letter and the Italian or italic script were formulated. With the new interest in calligraphy during the Renaissance and the demand for more manuscripts and scribes, many guides to calligraphy were written so that methods could be easily transmitted from one place to another. During the sixteenth century in England the growth of trade necessitated a rapidly written script, and the English commercial hand was created. This script became the model for most later writing systems, both in Europe and America. The illustration shows, from the top down, fifteenth-century Gothic, Chancery cursive, Cassinese, and English script.

In the Orient calligraphy has traditionally ranked more highly as an art form than it has in the West. The Chinese regard calligraphy as an art superior to painting, and works of the greatest calligraphers are valued as highly as are works of the greatest painters in the West. Because the Chinese system of calligraphy is far more complex than Western systems, it is far more demanding as well as allowing for greater creativity. The earliest Chinese script dates as far back as 1500 B.C.

The Islamic world has also always placed a high value on calligraphy. Part of this is because there was a long-time prohibition on representational art.

Western calligraphy developed from the Roman square capital from which developed the rustic capital written in a flowing style. Uncials or inch-high letters supplanted the two early forms. They were rounder and more inclined and more varied in size than the two previous lettering systems. From the half-uncial system developed a number of different writing styles current in various regions. Under Charlemagne an attempt was made to achieve a certain uniformity in calligraphy, and the great Carolingian script form was evolved. The Gothic script evolved thereafter but became highly elaborate and often diffi-

Callot Figures

Porcelain figures modeled after the engravings of grotesques by Jacques Callot (1592-1635). Callot, a French engraver and etcher, lived in Florence between 1612 and 1621. During his Florentine period he specialized in large crowd scenes, representations of dwarfs and hunchbacks, and drawings of *commedia dell'arte* figures. Callot displayed a technical virtuosity, liveliness of style, and mastery of composition that earned him a lasting popular influence. He is credited with raising etching from the mere reproduction of other works to an art in its own right. The famous dwarf subjects of his engravings were reproduced in porcelain factories in Meissen, Vienna, and Chelsea.

Cambric

A fabric named for the French city of Cambrai, its supposed place of origin. Cambric originally referred to a rather loosely woven linen, but the term was later extended to material of similar weave made of cotton.

Camelback

A chair back with three arches on its top rail. This design was used by both Chippendale and Hepplewhite for side chairs. The term also may have been applied to an eighteenth-century chair with a shield-shaped back.

Cameo

Principally, a jewelry term for carving done in low relief on a shell or striated stone with layers of two or more colors. A design is carved in a layer of one color with the other layer(s) left untouched to provide a contrasting background. In furniture design, *cameo* refers to decorations typically used on Adam and Sheraton pieces, and in Empire styles.

Cameo Glass

An ornamental glass in which layers of two different colors are fused and a relief design is carved from the upper layer. The most frequently used colors are white on blue. Cameo glass is used for jewelry and also for small decorative pieces such as vases.

Camouflage

Particularly in older apartments and houses, doors and windows are often awkwardly placed, rooms are poorly proportioned, and radiators and lighting fixtures seem to have been added as afterthoughts. You can disguise such unattractive features with camouflage, and make your home beautiful despite its structural faults. See *Camouflage,* p. 686.

Campaign Furniture

For centuries officers on military campaigns have furnished their quarters with lightweight chests and collapsible desks, chairs, and tables that were easy to pack and transport. Many contemporary pieces of similar design offer the same advantages to people who live in temporary homes. See *Campaign Furniture,* p. 689.

Candelabrum

In ancient Greece and Rome, a decorative candlestick or stand. Today the term chiefly refers to a heavily ornamented candlestick with two or more branches. It is also sometimes used interchangeably with chandelier to refer to a hanging ceiling light, and its plural form, *candelabra,* is often used in the singular.

Candles

To set a mood of friendly welcome, romantic mystery, or congenial warmth, there is nothing like the soft gleam of candlelight. Candles are available in an extravagant variety of lengths, shapes, colors, scents, and textures, and their decorative uses are legion. If you enjoy puttering with busywork projects, you can even make your own. See *Candles,* p. 690.

Candlewick Spread

Bedspread made of a fabric with a chenille-like appearance. Heavy pile yarn is used with surface loops cut to imitate true chenille yarn. The base fabric is usually an unbleached cotton muslin, to which "candlewick" yarn of single or mixed colors is added. This style of bedspread is frequently used with bedroom furnishings of American provincial style and informal character.

Cane bookcases and chairs in a contemporary room.

Cane

In furniture, wickerwork of split stems of certain palms, grasses, bamboo, or rattan, used for backs and seats of chairs. Caning was much used in the chair designs typical of the Louis XIV, XV, and XVI periods in France, in seventeenth-century designs in England and the Netherlands, and in many Oriental furniture designs. Today cane is a popular material for chairs for both indoor and outdoor use. It is also used for ornamental inserts for folding screens and a variety of casebuilt furniture. Cane pieces are equally attractive with a clear varnish finish or, as pictured here, painted in a striking color.

Canisters

A set of metal, ceramic, or wood containers customarily arranged on an open shelf in a kitchen for the storage of grocery staples, such as salt, sugar, and flour. Originally, a canister was a metal box for coffee or tea.

Canopies

In contemporary furnishings, the term *canopy* is ordinarily used to refer to a piece of overhead drapery, such as the covering of a four-poster bed. This design was introduced in the United States in the early nineteenth century and has remained popular. It is used especially in furniture of Early American and provincial styling, but also has a place in more formal designs for bedroom suites. See *Canopies,* p. 696; see also *Bedrooms,* Vol. 3.

Canterbury

A portable stand or rack now used primarily for the storage of magazines. It seems to have been named for an Archbishop of Canterbury who ordered a few of these pieces for his personal use. Evidently the pieces were used for various purposes: the storing of sheet music, the storing of periodicals, and the transporting of trays, cutlery, and plates.

Cantilever

A beam that projects beyond its vertical support, such as the wall of a building. A cantilever is usually used for the support of a balcony or other superimposed mass. It derives its support from the weight of the upper wall to which it is attached, or from some other counterweight.

The cantilever was originally made of stone, wood, or metal and was used widely in Gothic and early Renaissance buildings for the support of cornices, eaves, and balconies. Its use during the twentieth century is limited to buildings with steel frames and reinforced concrete structures.

Cantonnière

A valance-like bed hanging of French origin, dating from the sixteenth and seventeenth centuries, used for the canopy beds of members of the royal family and the nobility. The cantonnière was installed just below the upper

horizontal frame and was usually decorated with embroidery or material matching the other bed draperies. Its primary purpose was to keep out drafts at the points where the vertical draperies met at the bedposts.

Canvas

A firmly woven fabric usually made of cotton, linen, or hemp, used in decorating most commonly for awnings, drop curtains, wall panels, and upholstery for outdoor furniture. Contemporary decorators use canvas of awning quality in many innovative ways. Backed with a coating of liquid rubber, for example, it can make a practical floor covering.

Loosely woven canvas is employed as a backing for decorative needlework of many kinds. An extra-firm weave produces the fabric on which oil paintings are executed.

Canvas Panels

In furnishing attics or basements, canvas panels are ideal camouflage. Low in cost and easy to work with, they can hide many structural flaws and at the same time create new areas. See *Canvas Panels,* p. 700.

Capital

An architectural term for the head of a column, pillar, or shaft. In furniture design, capital forms have been used for their decorative value as well as for functional support. They were particularly popular in Renaissance and Louis XVI styles.

Capodimonte Porcelain

Porcelain of Italian and Spanish manufacture. The original Capodimonte factory was founded near Naples by King Charles III in 1743. After Charles became King of Spain in 1759, the factory was moved to Buen Retiro,

Canvas chair and rug in a contemporary room.

Capodimonte porcelain group with covered jar.

spindles. The sturdiness of the construction was intended to keep the chair upright as the ship moved across rough waters. Captain's chairs of lighter weight are frequently used today in the furnishing of dens and family rooms.

Caquetoire

A small, lightweight chair of sixteenth-century origin. The name is derived from the French word for chatter. Typically, the caquetoire has

a seat narrower at the back than at the front and arms that curve inward, from front to back, as shown in the sketch here.

Card Cut

Ornamental fretwork or lattice pattern, in low relief, used to decorate casebuilt furniture. Of Chinese origin, this decoration was used by Chippendale on cabinets and secretaries.

Card Table

A table designed to be used in the playing of a variety of games. Of unknown origin, the card or gaming table became extremely popular in eighteenth-century France and England. It was designed in a number of shapes and was given a variety of special features, the most common being a hinged top and corner sockets in which candles could be inserted. The most common covering for the playing surface was green baize. Many of the designs were quite elaborate.

near Madrid. The factory was returned to Naples where it continued its operations from 1773 to 1806. Because of the fineness of the porcelain and the quality of the decoration, Capodimonte porcelain has been widely imitated in figures, vases, jugs, and tableware. The pieces are often decorated with narrative scenes of classical origin or reproductions of paintings by famous contemporary artists.

Capriccio

Primarily an architectural term applying to fake ruins placed in gardens for picturesque effect. It is also applied to a kind of eighteenth-century Italian painting in which an architecturally accurate building is depicted in a dreamlike setting.

Captain's Chair

Low-backed armchair of heavy construction. The typical wooden captain's chair has a rounded back, at the top of which is a wide rail that extends around to the front, forming the arms of the chair. The saddle seat is connected to the rail by a series of rounded

Card table of inlaid cherry.

Most of today's card tables are plain, square tables that fold for storage and that have matching folding chairs. Some, however, are handsomely designed pieces suitable for permanent display.

Carpets and Rugs

The distinction between a carpet and a rug is somewhat obscure. The word *carpet* is often used generically to mean any fabric used as a floor covering, particularly that woven in widths and sewn together. The word *rug* usually implies a floor covering woven in a single piece of a particular shape. Generally the two words are used synonymously.

Floor coverings are among the most important items you will buy for your home, and they represent a major investment of your decorating dollars. Before shopping, you should know the advantages and disadvantages of the various sizes, colors, qualities, and textures available on today's market. See *Carpets and Rugs,* p. 704; see also *Accessories and Accents,* Vol. 1; *Floor Coverings,* Vol. 8; *Hooked Rugs,* Vol. 10; *Oriental Rugs,* Vol. 12.

Carports

Simple roofed structures with no siding can be satisfactory and relatively inexpensive substitutes for garages. If you have a carport attached to your house, it can often be converted into an extra room as your family and your income grow. See *Carports,* p. 710.

Carton-pierre

A type of papier-mâché developed by Robert Adam, one of four famous brothers who exerted great influence upon architecture and furniture design in England during the eighteenth century. The term translates literally from the French as stone cardboard. Carton-pierre was richly carved and decorated, then applied to interior walls and ceilings. Lighter than plaster, which was used for similar purposes, it was well suited to surfaces that could bear only a slight additional weight load.

Cartouche

A French term originally referring to a roll of paper containing gunpowder, taken over into architecture and furniture design to refer to an ornament in the form of a partially unrolled scroll or tablet with curled edges. Used as a central decorative feature on many Renais-

sance buildings, the cartouche was soon taken over for use on French and Italian furniture. The central plate was often decorated with arms or initials and was placed in a position of great importance. It was used from the fifteenth century on.

Cartwright, Edmund (1743-1823)

English inventor of the power loom, which was patented in 1785. The first crudely designed model was subsequently improved upon and was gradually developed into the modern power loom. The use of such looms revolutionized the textile industry, which had previously been based on hand weaving.

Carved Pile

Term applied to a type of carpeting with a surface pattern made by cutting the pile at different levels to create a sculptured appearance. The designs are most commonly scroll-like. Made of wool or synthetic materials, carved pile carpet is usually woven entirely from a single color.

Seventeenth-century Carver-style armchair. (Courtesy Metropolitan Museum of Art.)

Carver Chair

Armchair made of turned wood members, named after John Carver, the first governor of Plymouth Colony. The original Carver chair was said to have been brought over on the *Mayflower*. It formed the model for many early American chairs with its square shape, turned members, and vertical spindles. The three vertical spindles forming the back are connected by turned cross members top and bottom. The legs are also connected by turned members and are themselves turned. The top of the back is usually surmounted by mushroom-shaped finials, and the seat is ordinarily of cane or rush.

Carving

A term used in the decorative arts to denote forms or designs created by cutting. Although any kind of decorative scratching, incising, or chipping is considered carving, the two major types are low relief and high relief. These are distinguished by whether forms project from a surface less or more than half their thickness. Fully sculptured forms are sometimes referred to as carvings in the round, and cut decoration that penetrates a working surface is known as pierced or openwork carving.

Carving has always been a favorite method of furniture decoration, reflecting changing tastes throughout the centuries. The ancient Egyptians carved much of their wooden furniture with figures of animals, men, and gods, as did many ancient civilizations in the East. Indian, Japanese, and Chinese craftsmen have long been noted for their skill in carving leaf and flower forms, fantastic animals, and even entire landscapes.

In the West carved furniture has been popular in many periods. Gothic furniture often displays biblical scenes and figures carved on pews and benches made for churches and monasteries. During the Renaissance, decorative carving became a highly cultivated skill. Many fine pieces from the period have beautiful carvings of naturalistic garlands of fruit and flowers or figures and motifs from classical mythology. The taste for carved furniture pervaded Europe and in the Baroque era resulted in the extravagant ornamentation typical of many seventeenth-century pieces. Eighteenth-century fashions swung away from the heaviness of the Baroque toward lighter furniture styles, but in the nineteenth century Victorian tastes for massive solidity brought carved furniture once again into vogue. In contemporary times, tastes have once again reacted to the excesses of an earlier period. Moving away from the ostentatious and often crudely executed ornaments on Victorian furniture, modern furniture makers have largely rejected the whole concept of elaborate decoration and have sought functional solutions to design problems.

Caryatid

A carved female figure used as a decorative structural support. According to legend, a woman of the Caryae region in ancient Greece was turned into a walnut tree by the god Dionysus. Thus, in classical architecture the term *caryatid* came to be used to mean a statue of a draped female figure used as a supporting member.

The caryatid was taken over into furniture design in later centuries and was used in place of table and chair legs, pilasters of elaborate beds, mantels, and cabinets. First used during the Renaissance in Italy, it was also common on pieces made during the Jacobean, Francis I, Louis XIV, and Empire periods.

Cascaded Valance

A valance caught up at each edge at the top of the window, so that it falls in folds (cascades) over the draperies beneath to about a third of their length. This style is associated with fairly formal window treatments and is ordinarily used only for heavy or lined fabrics that will take on classic folds.

Caryatids on the Erechtheum, Athens, Greece.

Case Goods

A furniture trade term referring to all pieces that are of boxlike shape and function, such as chests, cupboards, bureaus, dressers, and cabinets. The essential property for furniture in this category is the ability to store things.

Quality in casebuilt pieces can be judged by both visible and hidden factors. Finish is the most obvious indication of quality; the best wood is kiln-dried. The highest quality veneer is five-ply, and three-ply material is considered adequate.

Drawer construction also reveals the quality of case goods. The best drawers open and close effortlessly and have concealed dovetail construction at both front and back. Drawer bottoms should be of substantial weight and should be grooved into side pieces. Small glue blocks at corners increase drawer strength and are an added indication of quality.

Casein Paint

Paint made with a casein solution mixed with water, noted for its quick-drying properties. The element in the paint that serves to cover the surface may be lime, powdered chalk, or kaolin. Also referred to as water-base paints, casein paints are particularly suitable for use on plaster walls and ceilings.

Casement Cloth

A sheer window curtain, either plain or figured and usually of solid, fairly neutral coloring. This is, however, a modern definition. The term has been used in various ways in the past. Since at one time the word *casement* was substituted for the word *window,* casement cloth has been used to refer to all kinds of curtains, drapery, and drapery linings.

Casement Window

In modern use, a window mounted on hinges that swings either in or out of the room as opposed to a window that is pushed up or down for opening or closing. As shown in the

sketch, casement windows are often decorated with casement cloth (glass curtains) hung from the top of the frame to the sill.

Cashmere

A very soft woolen fabric, or the yarn from which it is made. It is manufactured from the wool of an Indian goat and takes its name from the mountainous district of India to which the goat is native. Because of its softness and costliness, cashmere fabric is used only occasionally for decorating purposes.

Cassapanca

A long chest with a hinged top, a back, and arms. A combination of seat and locker, it was a popular item in mid-Renaissance Italian furniture and was usually heavily carved. The term is derived from the Italian *cassone,* which means chest or bench.

Cassolette

Originally a French word applying to a box or covered vase used for burning solid perfumes to sweeten the air. During the seventeenth century the term *brûle parfum* was used more widely. About the middle of the eighteenth century, however, the cassolette became an elaborate accessory used for decorative purposes. Often it was made in the shape of a classic urn or vase. Marble forms were overlaid with ormolu mountings. The cassolette also gained great popularity in England in the latter part of the eighteenth century.

Cast Iron

Iron containing 3.5 per cent of carbon, first made commercially by the Darby family in England in the early part of the eighteenth century. It was found that by smelting iron

ore with coke instead of charcoal it could be brought to a molten state suitable for pouring into casts. These cast-molded pieces—domes, columns, various architectural elements—became important in nineteenth-century building techniques. Cast iron has also been made into furniture forms, such as the chair illustrated here.

Casters

Small wheels on swivel bases installed on furniture legs for ease of movement. Also spelled castors.

Casual Furnishings

The province of casual living was once limited to the porch or the lawn. Today informality is a keynote of life both in and out of doors, and the modern homemaker is well advised to consider informal furnishings that are easy to maintain and suitable to a life style that does not include the help of household servants. See *Casual Furnishings,* p. 716; see also *Indoor-Outdoor Relationships,* Vol. 10.

Cathedral Ceiling

A high-pitched ceiling, often decorated with exposed beams. This type of ceiling is used in contemporary homes, especially in the extra-high living rooms that are a feature of split-level designs.

Caucasian Rugs

Carpets woven by nomads and villagers who live in the Caucasus, a rough mountainous area of western Russia. Typified by strong, bright colors and striking geometric motifs and patterns, Caucasian rugs are noted for

Caucasian rug from Kuba.

energetic and powerful designs. Many general design-types are known, named for the villages or areas where they were made or for the peoples who made them. Among the better known are Kuba, and Kasak (Cossack).

Causeuse

A small sofa, resembling the modern love seat, of seventeenth- or eighteenth-century origin. It has an upholstered seat and back, and open sides. The name comes from the French verb *causer* meaning to chat.

Cavetto

Decorative molding of concave form used either as a member of a cornice or, in late-seventeenth-century English furniture, as a crosswise veneered edging across the upper portion of a casebuilt piece.

Cedar

The wood from any of several members of the conifer family. Because of its durability and its sweet-smelling, insect-repelling qualities, it is widely used in the construction of closets, or for the lining of closets or clothing chests. The most common forms of cedar are of a reddish color. The African cedar, wine-red in color, was used extensively by French cabinet-makers. The use of cedar dates back to ancient times. Because of its supposed everlasting quality, it was used by the Romans for the carving of statues of the gods.

Cedar Chest

A closed chest made from or lined with cedar. Usually low, long, and top-opening, cedar chests have traditionally been used for the storage of clothing and linens. The proverbial "hope chest" was usually made of cedar and was used for the storage of garments and linens for girls to bring with them upon marriage. In earlier times cedar chests were often elaborately carved, and they are made today to suit any period or style of furniture.

Ceilings

Overhead decoration has been a part of many historic styles of architecture and furnishing. Peoples of widely different cultures all over the world have embellished the ceilings of their homes, palaces, and places of worship with painted, sculptural, and structural ornaments, designs, and pictures. A revival of interest in the decorative value of ceilings has occurred in contemporary times, and modern designers recommend that the home decorator take a good look not only around but up as well. Exposed beams, textured plaster, tile, planking, and patterned paper and fabric can all be used to add ceiling interest to your home. See *Ceilings,* p. 718; see also *Beamed Ceilings,* Vol. 3, and *Sound Control,* Vol. 15.

Celadon

Any of a variety of Oriental porcelains characterized by a gray-green glaze and smooth velvety texture. For hundreds of years particularly fine porcelain of this type was made at

Korean celadon incense burner.

various kilns in China and Korea. Much was exported to Europe, where the ware became known as celadon during the seventeenth century and was widely imitated by ceramists in many countries from the eighteenth century onward.

Celanese

The trade name used by the Celanese Corporation of America for its rayon fiber or fabric.

Cellarette

Originally, the portion of a sideboard in which wine bottles and decanters were stored. In eighteenth-century furniture design the term was applied to a small, portable cabinet for wine and glassware storage. Usually of mahogany or rosewood, this type of cellarette was commonly many-sided in shape. Zinc or lead lining was often used to provide a cool storage area for the wines, and the interior was sometimes partitioned to form wine racks.

Contemporary room ceiled with cellulose panels.

Cellulose

Chemically, any one of a large number of acetic esters—insoluble starch substances obtained from plants. Today cellulose is used as a basis for synthetic fibers and yarns that go into the manufacture of a wide variety of materials. Cellulose products are also combined with natural fibers to create still other materials.

Centerpieces

Table decoration has traditionally focused on centerpieces of flowers, fruit, foliage, and candles, but all sorts of accessories can be teamed with them for added interest. Flowers are not really difficult to arrange attractively and are almost everybody's first choice for a beautiful centerpiece. Fruit has the advantage of being dessert as well as decoration, and even vegetables can be charming on a table. What you put on your table or buffet can often be the final perfect touch that will complement your food and please your guests. See *Centerpieces,* p. 730; see also *Flower Arrangements,* Vol. 8, and *Table Settings and Linens,* Vol. 16.

Centers of Interest

Any good composition has a center of interest, a place that immediately attracts attention and is the focal point of an overall scheme. Every well-decorated room has one, and any home decorator can easily create one. All it takes is a little thought and planning. See *Centers of Interest,* p. 738; see also *Accessories and Accents,* Vol. 1; *Collections,* Vol. 5; and *Furniture Arrangement,* Vol. 9.

Ceramics

Objects made of clay or similar materials and fired to fix their shape. The variety of production techniques and decorative styles is immense. Among the most common types included in the category of ceramics are bone china, porcelain, earthenware, and stoneware.